101 Rhythm Instrument Activities
for Young Children

Dedication

To the memory of my mother, Elizabeth Terpenning Flesch, who always encouraged and supported my creativity.

101 Rhythm Instrument Activities for Young Children

Abigail Flesch Connors
Illustrated by Deborah C. Wright

Gryphon House, Inc.
Lewisville, NC

© 2004 Abigail Flesch Connors
Published by Gryphon House, Inc.
PO Box 10, Lewisville, NC 27023
800.638.0928 (toll free); 877.638.7576 (fax)

Visit us on the web at www.gryphonhouse.com

Cover illustration: Joan Waites
Illustrations: Deborah C. Wright

Reprinted July 2013

Library of Congress Cataloging-in-Publication Data

Connors, Abigail Flesch, 1957-
    101 rhythm instrument activities for young children / by Abigail
Flesch Connors ; illustrations, Deborah C. Wright.
        p. cm.
Includes indexes.
  ISBN 978-0-87659-290-8
  1. Rhythm--Study and teaching (Preschool) 2. Education,
Preschool--Activity programs. 3. Music in education. I. Title: One
hundred one rhythm instrument activities for young children. II. Title:
One hundred and one rhythm instrument activities for young children.
III. Title.
  GV463.C66 2004
  372.87--dc22
                                                        2003016466

Bulk purchase
Gryphon House books are available at special discount when purchased in bulk for special premiums and sales promotions as well as for fund-raising use. Special editions or book excerpts also can be created to specification. For details, contact the Director of Marketing.

Disclaimer
The publisher and the author cannot be held responsible for injury, mishap, or damages incurred during the use of or because of the activities in this book. The author recommends appropriate and reasonable supervision at all times based on the age and capability of each child. Every effort has been made to locate copyright and permission information.

Table of Contents

Introduction. 7

**10 Classroom Management Tips for
    Using Rhythm Instruments . . . 10**

Activities Using Rhythm Sticks . . 13

1. Rhythm Sticks Introduction 14
2. Different Ways to Play Sticks 15
3. This Is The Way We Tap Our Sticks 15
4. Sticks Up And Down 16
5. The Sticks on the Bus 17
6. If You're Happy and You Know It
   Tap Your Sticks 18
7. Walk in the Woods 18
8. Rainstorm. 20
9. BINGO Sticks 20
10. London Bridge Letters 21
11. We Are Tapping 22
12. Tapping or Scraping? 22
13. Conducting Sticks 23
14. Copy My Rhythm 23
15. Everybody Count to Six 24
16. I Am a Fine Musician 24
17. Old King Cole's Sticks 25
18. Guess Who Tapped? 25
19. The Tapper in the Dell 26
20. The Sticks Are Going for a Walk 26
21. Don't Say Ain't 27
22. Shapes With Sticks 27
23. Experiments With Sticks 28
24. Standing With Sticks 28
25. Trot, Gallop, Freeze! 29

26. The Cat and the Mouse 29
27. Hot Cross Buns 31
28. Windshield Wipers 31
29. The Spider Went Over the Spider Web . 32
30. Beethoven's 5th Symphony 32
31. Jack and Jill 33
32. "Painting" on the Floor 33
33. Tap, Tap, Tap Your Boat 34

Activities Using Shakers 35

34. Shakers Introduction 36
35. Different Ways to Play Shakers 37
36. Going to Kentucky 37
37. Waltz of the Flowers 38
38. Wake Up, Groundhog! 39
39. Experiments With Shakers 39
40. This Is the Way We Clean the House . . . 40
41. Wind Song 41
42. Ocean Waves 41
43. Stir Up My Soup 42
44. Shake It High and Shake It Low 42
45. Shaker Square Dance 43
46. Digging Up a Hole 44
47. Little Baby. 45
48. The Animals in the Jungle 46
49. Where Is Shaker? 47
50. Shaker Parade 48
51. Who Will Help Me?
    (The Little Red Hen) 48
52. Shakers Count to Ten 49
53. Teddy Bear Shakers 49
54. I'm a Little Raindrop 50

Activities Using Jingle Bells 51

55. Jingle Bells Introduction 52

56. Different Ways to Play Bells 53

57. Jingle Bells 53

58. Little Jingle Mouse 54

59. We're Passing Around the Bells 54

60. Twinkle, Twinkle, Little Star 55

61. Bells or Shaker? 55

62. Bells in Socks 56

63. Bells on Ankles 56

64. Freeze Dance With Bells 57

65. Jingle at the Window 57

66. Hickory Dickory Dock 58

67. Circus Tricks With Bells 59

68. Jingle Around the Rosie 59

69. Frère Jacques 60

70. All About Colors 61

71. Nice and Warm 62

Activities Using Sand Blocks 63

72. Sand Blocks Introduction 64

74. The Train Is Coming 65

73. Different Ways to Play Sand Blocks 65

75. The Train Is Going Up the Hill 66

76. Engine, Engine, Number Nine 67

77. The Sand Blocks Went to a Party 67

78. Happy Birthday Cha-Cha-Cha 68

79. In the Middle of the Night 69

80. Go 'Round and 'Round the Village 70

81. Sand Blocks Like to Clap 70

Activities Using Other Instruments 73

82. Cymbals Introduction 74

83. New Year's Eve Countdown 75

84. Pop Goes the Weasel 75

85. Introduction to the Drum 76

86. The Drum Game 77

87. Animal Footsteps 77

88. All About the Triangle 78

89. All About the Tambourine 78

90. Tambourine Walk 79

Rhythm Band Activities 81

91. Old MacDonald's Instruments 82

92. The Instruments on the Bus 83

93. Rig-a-Jig-Jig 83

94. Freeze Parade 84

95. Rock-a-Bye Baby 85

96. The Instruments in the Dell 85

97. She'll Be Tapping 'Round the Mountain (Rhythm Band) 86

98. Do You Know the Jingle Bells? 87

99. Conducting the Rhythm Band 88

100. Where Are the Sand Blocks? 89

101. Simon Says 90

Good Activities for Toddlers 91

Subject Index 93

Seasons Index 95

Monthly Planning Pages for Rhythm Instrument Activities . 99

Index III

Introduction

As soon as babies are able to hold objects, they start to bang them, shake them, and throw them on the floor. They do this to learn about their bodies' capabilities, to explore their environment, and to test the properties of physical objects, but most of all, they do this to experience the joy of creating sounds. What a wonderful feeling it is when they discover that they can make noise in so many ways! It's a feeling of wonder, delight, and power. To paraphrase seventeenth century philosopher René Descartes, the baby's philosophy is: "I'm LOUD, therefore I am!"

As early childhood teachers, our goal must be to respect and satisfy children's need to make noise, while gently guiding them toward expressing themselves musically.

Rhythm instruments provide a uniquely effective medium to bridge this gap. Children respond to rhythm sticks, shakers, and other instruments with instinctive enthusiasm. They literally celebrate life with a bang (and a shake, rattle, and roll)! And when you use rhythm instruments in the context of songs, stories, and musical games, children develop an awareness of rhythm, phrasing, tempo, and other elements of musicality. It's an incredible joy to see children discover the music within themselves!

You know how important music is for young children. I'm not just referring to its role in the development of many kinds of intelligence—which has been well documented—but the sheer joy of experiencing music. For socialization and a feeling of belonging, nothing compares with the bond that is formed when a group makes music together. Shy children will start to come out of their shells a bit to join in, and aggressive children will cooperate so they can take part in the fun. Music, a natural outlet for creativity and self-expression, is a basic human need. Yet some children don't even realize that music is something they can create. Once I was singing a song with a group of children and a little girl asked, "But where's the *music*, Miss Abby? Where's the *music*?" She was looking around me and behind me. It took me a moment to realize that she meant, "Where's the CD?" She was bewildered by the idea of people making their own music!

For many of you, the most basic, natural way to express musical ideas is through singing, and I encourage a lot of singing. The problem is that not all children will participate in singing activities. Some children live in homes where there isn't a lot of singing, and some are just naturally shy or self-conscious. There are many reasons why a child may not feel comfortable singing in a group.

Another problem in preschool is that singing often occurs in the context of learning a new song, which is a hard thing for many young children. Learning a new song involves listening, remembering words, understanding words, pronouncing words, remembering and singing a tune—quite a lot of skills.

In contrast, rhythm instrument activities are *so* easy! Most of them involve simply copying one motion at a time. There's nothing to remember. Also, there's no right or wrong way to do it, which leaves plenty of room for individuality.

Another wonderful thing about rhythm instruments is that they involve the *body* in keeping a beat and feeling rhythm. The children are fully participating musically. They're really creating music, without even trying!

Rhythm instrument activities both reinforce and build *body awareness*, as you use different parts of the body ("Let's shake it on our arms; let's shake it behind our backs"). They build *spatial awareness* as you move the instruments through space in various directions and with big and small ranges of motion. It encourages *movement exploration* and expands your *movement repertoire and vocabulary*. For instance, a child may not have performed a certain movement before, such as turning a shaker around or shaking it upside down. As the children experience the new movement, I verbalize it ("Now you're turning your shaker around") so that the vocabulary stays with them—because they're *doing* it while they're hearing the words.

These activities also promote *understanding of concepts* such as up and down, over and under, high and low, soft and loud, short and long, in and out, and stop and go.

With all of these possibilities, rhythm instruments are truly an extraordinary learning tool, and they're so much fun!

During more than 12 years as an early childhood music specialist, I've taught rhythm instrument activities to toddlers, preschoolers, and kindergarteners; in small groups and large groups; in all kinds of settings. One thing is true everywhere I go—kids love playing rhythm instruments!

I've found rhythm instrument games and activities to be so enjoyable—for the children I teach and for myself—that I've often wondered: Why don't more teachers of young children use rhythm instruments on a regular basis? I believe that the only reason is that there is simply a lack of resources for teaching rhythm instrument activities.

I'm constantly scouring libraries, bookstores, and catalogs for any and all teaching materials relating to music and young children. Although many excellent books, recordings, and videos are out there, I have never found a single book devoted to the use of rhythm instruments with groups of young children.

I noticed that preschool children in my class were very curious and excited about rhythm instruments and wanted to play them more than just once in a while. They taught me, with their inspiring inventiveness and imagination, that there was a lot more to experience and explore with rhythm instruments!

That's when I began to develop my own rhythm instruments curriculum—to help children explore the sound and movement possibilities of playing rhythm instruments. I created this book to share these activities with preschool teachers and others who are looking for meaningful musical experiences for their classes. It's a selection of activities for many kinds of rhythm instruments. Some activities are my original creations; some are adapted from traditional songs and stories. You'll find activities for rhythm sticks, shakers (maracas), jingle bells, sand blocks, and many other instruments.

Quality rhythm instruments are readily available and (with some exceptions) usually quite inexpensive. Many rhythm instruments are easy to make as a class project, costing little or nothing! (See *Rubber-Band Banjos and a Java Jive Bass: Projects and Activities on the Science of Music and Sound* by Alex Sabbeth, published by John Wiley, 1997.) Recordings and instruments can be found in school supply stores and catalogs, in bookstores, and on websites.

This isn't the kind of book where you need to start at the beginning and go through to the end. For instance, you may decide one day that you haven't used rhythm sticks in a while, so you could just turn to that section and choose an activity. Or you may be teaching a unit on weather, shapes, trains, or whatever, and you could turn to the **Seasons Index** or **Subject Index** for an appropriate activity. (Hopefully, you will enjoy looking through the whole book at some point, too!)

These activities are so easy to do! You don't need a lot of space or a lot of time. You don't need to read music or prepare materials or even practice—you can just open this book and start using it.

Most of the activities here are suitable for children ages 3-6, but many are also appropriate for children as young as 18 months (see the section **Good Activities for Toddlers**).

Music is a vital part of children's lives, and when they can make music themselves it is immensely satisfying for them. I know you'll have a great time sharing their joy and excitement! Have fun!

10 Classroom Management Tips for Using Rhythm Instruments

1 Tell children to keep their hands in their laps when you are passing out instruments. If you have a very rambunctious group, try playing "Simon Says" while you pass out instruments. While the children sit in the circle, say, "Simon says touch your ears…" "Simon says touch your nose…" "Simon says clap your hands…" and so on. This will keep their attention focused (and their hands busy!) for a minute.

2 Another good distraction while you're passing out instruments is to ask, "What if?" questions. For example, "What if the instruments were made of glass? What would happen?" "What if they were made of paper?" "What if the instruments were teeny-tiny? Who could play them?"

3 Using child "helpers" to pass out instruments actually can be very helpful! The first few times, select children who are fairly responsible and good at following directions. Explain that they should pass out the instruments in order, not to their best friends first. Keep a chart or list of helpers so that everyone gets a turn.

4 Make it a rule that children do not pick up instruments until you tell them that they may. It is a good idea to take an instrument away from a child who is not listening, but return it as soon as possible to give him or her another opportunity to listen (and have fun!).

5 Make sure the children have enough space to play their instruments freely. Try to have "breathing room" between children. Also, if possible, position the group so that no one is backed up against a wall or toy shelf.

6 Make sure everyone in the group can see your face and hear what you're saying.

7 Emphasize the correct position for playing instruments. I used to do too much "don't"-ing: "Don't bang it too hard," "Don't play it near your face," and so on, until all the children would chime in with their suggestions for more rules. One little girl said, "And you should never put it inside your nose!" (I hadn't thought of that one!)

8 As further incentive to handle instruments carefully, talk about what the instruments are made of—usually wood, metal, or hard plastic. Pointing this out makes children less likely to be careless.

9 If your group doesn't respond well to word signals, try sound signals such as a whistle, kazoo, or bell to signal it's time to stop playing. You can make a game out of practicing this for a while. Ask the children to play their instruments, and see who can respond the fastest to the sound signal to stop. This is one of those "tricks" that can really work wonders.

10 The best management technique of all is to be totally focused on the activity. Show enthusiasm and build anticipation. If YOU are involved, the children will be involved too!

Activities Using Rhythm Sticks

I always introduce rhythm sticks before the other instruments. It seems like the natural thing to do because their sound, unlike the other instruments, makes a very clear, sharp beat. In the developmental journey from noise to music, the beat is like a road, or a track, that keeps you together, headed in the right direction. The hard tap of wood on wood offers an easy-to-hear beat.

The sticks I use with my classes are the wooden kind, which are generally sold in pairs of one smooth and one fluted (with ridges). With this combination, you can scrape the fluted stick with the smooth stick to make an interesting sound, which is featured in many of the following activities.

A word of advice: If you're purchasing rhythm sticks for the first time, try to specify that they are all the same color. If the sticks are different colors, some children may get distracted and ask for particular colors or if they can trade sticks with a friend. Without the color issue, children are free to focus on the musical activity.

So get ready to tap, scrape, hammer, pound, click, and have a great time exploring the sounds of rhythm sticks!

Rhythm Sticks Introduction

If you're hesitant to put large sticks in the hands of preschoolers, you should be! Rhythm sticks are wonderful musical instruments for young children, but they do need to be introduced carefully and thoughtfully.

It can be helpful to teach an introductory lesson using one pair of sticks. Show the children how to hold the sticks, with your forearms resting on your thighs (when sitting cross-legged on the floor, this automatically puts your sticks in a good position) and your hands just a few inches off the floor. Tap the sticks together gently, using only a small wrist motion. You may want to have the children practice this motion a few times without the instruments. Explain that it's not necessary to bang the sticks hard to get a nice loud sound.

Then pass the sticks around the circle and let each child practice proper position and gentle tapping.

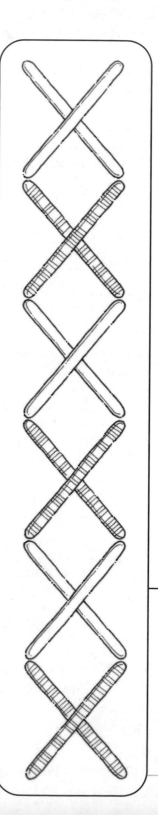

Different Ways to Play Sticks

Put on a tape of rhythmic instrumental music, such as a march or anything with a strong, steady beat. Encourage the children to copy you as you play the sticks in different ways. Here are some ideas to get you started:

- tap the sticks together
- tap the floor—sticks together
- tap the floor, alternating right and left sticks
- scrape the sticks together
- "roll" the sticks (hold the sticks waist high, parallel to the ground and pointing towards each other, and roll them around each other with a cranking motion)
- tap your shoes with the sticks
- tap your knees (gently!) with the sticks
- "hammer"—hold one stick vertically on the ground and "hammer" the top with the other stick
- hold the tops of the sticks and pound them vertically on the floor

Variation: Play "Copy the Child." This game can be played two different ways: you can ask two or three children to have turns of about 30 seconds each to lead the group, or you can go around the circle and let each child do a different motion for the group to copy. (I love this kind of activity because it stimulates the children's creativity. I'm always amazed at the inventiveness of their ideas!)

This game can also be played with shakers, bells, or other instruments.

This Is the Way We Tap Our Sticks

Sing the following song to the tune of "Here We Go 'Round the Mulberry Bush":

This is the way we tap our sticks,
Tap our sticks, tap our sticks.
This is the way we tap our sticks,
So early in the morning.

Tap your sticks to the beat while singing the verse.

Then show the children how to rub the smooth stick across the top of the bumpy stick, in an outward motion, to make a scraping sound. Sing:

This is the way we scrape our sticks…

Additional verses:

This is the way we tap them soft… (tap very softly)

This is the way we scrape them soft… (scrape very softly)

This is the way we tap the floor… (tap the floor with both sticks)

This is the way we tap our shoes… (put feet out in front and gently tap shoes with sticks)

Here's a special way to "scrape them loud": Hold the bumpy stick against the floor while scraping it with the smooth stick. Sound travels faster through solids than through the air, and this makes a *huge* sound when a roomful of children do it together. Needless to say, this is a very popular activity!

Sticks Up and Down

This game teaches how to pay careful attention, a skill that the children will need later for more involved activities.

It is actually an introduction to something they'll be doing in almost every rhythm instrument activity: Following your directions for picking up the instruments and for putting them down.

Give each child a pair of rhythm sticks, one plain and one fluted (I call them "smoothies" and "bumpies"). The children should keep their hands in their laps until you ask them to pick up their sticks.

Explain that you will say, "Pick up your sticks" and pick up your own sticks when it is time for them to do so, and that you'll say, "And down," while gently lowering your sticks to the floor, to signal when it's time for them to put their sticks down. This may sound basic, but it's very important for them to know and follow

your signals. These will be your signals for every time you play with instruments. To play this game, put on some moderately lively music with a steady beat. Practice the "pick up" signal, tap the sticks to the beat, and then practice "and down." Continue for a few minutes.

Remind the children to keep their hands in their laps while you collect the sticks.

The Sticks on the Bus

This is an easy and fun game for the children to practice different stick techniques.

Sing the following song to the tune of "The Wheels on the Bus":

The sticks on the bus go tap, tap, tap;
Tap, tap, tap; tap, tap, tap.
The sticks on the bus go tap, tap, tap
All through the town.

Tap your sticks to the beat.

Additional verses:

The sticks on the bus go scrape, scrape, scrape…

The sticks on the bus go pound, pound, pound… (pound sticks vertically on floor)

The sticks on the bus go hammer, hammer, hammer…

The sticks on the bus go roll, roll, roll…

If You're Happy and You Know It Tap Your Sticks

Sing the following song to the tune of "If You're Happy and You Know It Clap Your Hands":

If you're happy and you know it tap your sticks. (tap, tap)
If you're happy and you know it tap your sticks. (tap, tap)
If you're happy and you know it,
Then your face will surely show it,
If you're happy and you know it tap your sticks. (tap, tap).

Emphasize the two-beat "tap, tap" at the end of the first, second, and fifth lines.

Additional verses:

If you're happy and you know it tap them soft…

If you're happy and you know it scrape your sticks…

If you're happy and you know it scrape them soft…

If you're happy and you know it scrape them loud…(hold the fluted stick against the floor and scrape it with the other stick)

Walk in the Woods

This is a sound story that you can dramatize using rhythm sticks. It's a little bit scary—in a fun way, of course—but may be too scary for some three-year-olds. (I use it with Pre-K and kindergarten groups.)

Tell the following story while tapping your sticks as indicated, encouraging the children to follow along with their sticks.

Before you begin, ask the children to pick up their sticks and be ready to play.

One day I went for a walk in the woods. It was very dark and very quiet. All of a sudden I heard some slow footsteps behind me—tap… tap… tap… tap… tap… tap… (children should join in the slow rhythm).

After a while the footsteps got a little faster, like this: tap-tap… tap-tap… tap-tap… tap-tap… I was a little scared because I didn't know what it was, but I kept walking (tap sticks faster to the rhythm).

Then the footsteps got even faster, like this: tap tap, tap tap, tap tap, tap tap, tap tap… I got really scared, but I just had to know what it was! So I turned around to look (turn head slowly) *and I saw that it was…… a bear! So I ran home as fast as I could* (tap sticks very fast)!

The End! And down (lower sticks to the floor).

Children will want to play this again and again. Encourage them to come up with new ideas for different animals to meet in the woods. They'll often request lions, dinosaurs, and other scary animals, but sometimes someone will ask to meet a kitten or a bunny rabbit. If so, you might suggest a different ending, such as, "So I said, 'hi' to the cute little kitten."

Rainstorm (Sticks)

This sound story is lots of fun anytime, but especially on a rainy day!

Before you begin the story, ask the children to hold their sticks without playing them yet.

One day I was sitting in my house. It was very quiet. All of a sudden, I heard some light raindrops on my roof. They sounded like this (tap sticks softly and very slowly).

After a while the rain got a little heavier (tap a bit louder and faster), and then a little heavier, and then it turned into a rainstorm (tap very fast for a while)! And then it stopped (stop tapping). And down (lay sticks on the floor).

This activity is great for introducing the concept of *acceleration*, or becoming faster little by little. Preschoolers tend to think in terms of two speeds: slow and fast. This game helps them to understand the idea of music and rhythms getting faster a little bit at a time.

BINGO Sticks

The clapping song "B-I-N-G-O" is ideal for use with rhythm sticks. Instead of clapping, just tap!

There was a farmer had a dog, and Bingo was his name-o,
B-I-N-G-O, B-I-N-G-O, B-I-N-G-O, and Bingo was his name-o.

Continue singing the following verses and tapping as indicated:

There was a farmer had a dog, and Bingo was his name-o,
(tap)-I-N-G-O, (tap)-I-N-G-O…

There was a farmer had a dog, and Bingo was his name-o,
(tap, tap)-*N-G-O*, (tap, tap)-*N-G-O*…

There was a farmer had a dog, and Bingo was his name-o,
(tap, tap, tap)-*G-O*, (tap, tap, tap)-*G-O*…

There was a farmer had a dog, and Bingo was his name-o,
(tap, tap, tap, tap)-*O*, (tap, tap, tap, tap)-*O*…

There was a farmer had a dog, and Bingo was his name-o,
(tap, tap, tap, tap, tap), (tap, tap, tap, tap, tap)…

London Bridge Letters

Children often try to make letter shapes using the rhythm sticks, so I decided to make a song out of it. You can introduce this activity by telling the children that the rhythm sticks don't just make music, they can also make letters of the alphabet!

Sing the following song to the tune of "London Bridge Is Falling Down":

> *I can make the letter T,*
> *Letter T, letter T,*
> *I can make the letter T,*
> *With my sticks.*

Ask the children to try to make the letter T with their sticks, either flat on the floor or standing up. Each child will probably want you to admire his or her T, so take some time to do so.

You can also make (and sing about) the letters V, L, and (not quite as easily) X.

Discuss why they can't make all of the letters of the alphabet with the sticks. Ask them, "Why can't you make the letter A?" (Not enough sticks.) "Why can't you make a B?" (Too curvy—sticks are straight lines.)

Children may want to try making more letters by using more than two sticks. Encourage their efforts and see what they can come up with!

We Are Tapping

This is another activity that uses a variety of stick techniques.

Sing the following song to the tune of "Clementine":

> *We are tapping, we are tapping,*
> *We are tapping with our sticks.*
> *We are tapping, we are tapping,*
> *We are tapping with our sticks.*

Additional verses:

> *We are scraping…*

> *We are hammering…*

> *We are pounding…*

> *We are rolling…*

Note that the "Clementine" tune is in ¾ time—three beats to a measure. Emphasize the first beat of each measure so the children can follow the rhythm more easily: *We are tap-ping, we are tap-ping…*

Tapping or Scraping?

This is a fun listening activity. Listening is an important part of music (perhaps *the* most important part), and careful listening is a skill that can be developed with practice.

This activity is a "confidence builder," not a challenge. It gets children into the habit of careful listening.

Only the teacher has sticks for this activity. The children sit in a circle, and you sit in the middle. Ask one child at a time to turn away from the circle and close his or her eyes. Tap or scrape the rhythm sticks and ask the child to say whether you tapped or scraped. Do this with each child in the circle.

Be sure to notice what good listeners they are!

Conducting Sticks

Tell the children that today you will be a conductor—a person who leads a group of musicians. Explain that you will show them how to play their rhythm sticks by using hand signals. You will bring your hands up, palms facing up, to tell them to tap loudly. You will bring your hands down, palms facing down, to tell them to play softly.

Practice a few times without music, and then put on some music that has a steady rhythm. Lead the group in playing loudly and softly. Go from very loud to very soft, and everywhere in between!

Then let the children take turns being the conductor. They'll love the experience of directing a roomful of sound using only their hands!

Copy My Rhythm

This activity can be tricky—it involves careful listening, observing, and playing.

The teacher holds one pair of sticks. Pass another pair of sticks around the circle to give each child a turn.

Tap a rhythm on your sticks. (Keep it simple!) Then ask the child with the sticks to try to copy it. Give the child several tries if needed.

Here are some ideas for easy rhythms (don't sing or say them aloud, just tap the rhythm):

> Hap-py birth-day to you…
> Lon-don Bridge is fal-ling down…
> Ring a-round the ro-sie…
> It-sy bit-sy spi-der…
> Jin-gle bells, jin-gle bells…
> Jack and Jill went up the hill…
> Row, row, row your boat…
> Oh say can you see…
> Ee-ny mee-ny mi-ny moe…
> Hick-o-ry Dick-o-ry Dock…

Or make up rhythms of your own, but keep them short and simple.

Everybody Count to Six

Sing the following song to the tune of the first two lines of "Twinkle, Twinkle, Little Star" (repeated) while tapping your sticks on the beats of the numbers (lines 2 and 4):

Everybody count to six,
One, two, three, four, five, six.
Tap to six upon your sticks,
One, two, three, four, five, six.

Additional verses (change only the third line):

Scrape to six upon your sticks…

Pound to six upon your sticks…

Hammer to six upon your sticks…

I Am a Fine Musician

This traditional song is easily adapted to rhythm sticks.
Tap to the beat while singing.

I am a fine musician,
That's what people say.
And people come from all around
Just to hear me play.
My tapping, my tapping,
They love to hear my tapping.
I am a fine musician,
That's what people say.

Additional verses (same as above except lines 5 and 6):

My scraping, my scraping, they love to
*   hear my scraping…*

My hammering, my hammering, they love to hear my hammering…

My pounding, my pounding, they love to hear my pounding…

Old King Cole's Sticks

Sing the following song while tapping your sticks to the beat:

> *Old King Cole was a merry old soul,*
> *And a merry old soul was he.*
> *He called for his pipe, and he called for his bowl,*
> *And he called for his tappers three.*
> *And his tappers three went tap, tap, tap,*
> *Tap, tap, tap, tap, tap.*

Additional verses (same as above except lines 4, 5, and 6):

> *And he called for his scrapers three.*
> *And his scrapers went scrape, scrape, scrape,*
> *Scrape, scrape, scrape, scrape, scrape.*

> *And he called for his hammerers three.*
> *And his hammerers went hammer, hammer, hammer,*
> *Hammer, hammer, hammer, hammer, hammer.*

> *And he called for his pounders three.*
> *And his pounders went pound, pound, pound,*
> *Pound, pound, pound, pound, pound.*

Guess Who Tapped?

This is a moderately difficult listening game.

Each child has a pair of sticks in front of him or her. Go around the circle, giving each child a turn if time permits. Ask one child to turn away from the circle and close his or her eyes. The teacher silently points to another child in the circle. This child picks up the sticks, taps a few times, and puts the sticks back down. Then the first child turns around to guess who tapped the sticks. (You may want to give the child three tries.)

Encourage the children to listen to where the sound seems to be coming from.

The Tapper in the Dell

Tap to the beat while you sing the following song to the tune of "The Farmer in the Dell":

> *The tapper in the dell,*
> *The tapper in the dell,*
> *Hi-ho, the derry-o,*
> *The tapper in the dell.*

Additional verses:

> *The scraper in the dell…*
> *The hammerer in the dell…*
> *The pounder in the dell…*
> *The roller in the dell…*

The Sticks Are Going for a Walk

Show the children how to hold the tops of their sticks and gently "walk" them on the floor (while sitting). Do this while singing the following song to the tune of "Here We Go 'Round the Mulberry Bush":

> *The sticks are going for a walk,*
> *For a walk, for a walk,*
> *The sticks are going for a walk,*
> *So early in the morning.*

Additional verses:

> *The sticks are going on tippy-toe…* ("walk" sticks lightly and delicately)

> *The sticks are going running today…* ("walk" sticks quickly)

> *The sticks are going skiing today…* (hold sticks flat and "ski" them back and forth on the floor)

> *The sticks are going jumping today…* (hold tops of sticks and "jump" them gently on the floor)

Don't Say Ain't

I don't know where this rhyme comes from, but it seems to have been around forever. (Maybe it's an old jump rope rhyme?) And children love it!

As you chant the following rhyme, tap on the dominant beats (in boldface type):

> **Don't say ain't.**
> Your **mother will faint.**
> Your **father will step** in a **bucket of paint.**
> Your **sis**ter will cry.
> Your **bro**ther will sigh.
> The **cat** and the **dog will say good-bye!**

When the children are familiar with the rhyme, you can try tapping and chanting it in different ways: slow, fast, soft, loud, in a low voice, in a high squeaky voice, and so on.

Shapes With Sticks

Each child has a pair of sticks. Put the children into groups of two and ask them to try to form triangles with their sticks. Then discuss what happened. "How many sticks did you need? Why?"

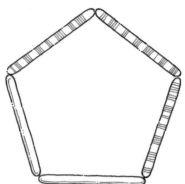

Now ask the children to try to make squares with their sticks. Discuss how they made them. Ask the children why they can't make circles with their sticks. (Some children may think they can!) "Are there any other shapes you could make with the rhythm sticks?" (If you have a really interested group, you might want to teach them about pentagons, rectangles, or diamonds.)

Experiments With Sticks

This is a sound exploration activity. Each child has a pair of sticks. Pass around a folded sheet of newspaper and let each child have a turn tapping on it.

Then ask, "What if you crumple up the newspaper? Will it sound different when you tap on it?" Try it.

Try tapping on:

- flat aluminum foil
- crumpled aluminum foil
- flat pieces of cardboard
- cardboard boxes
- wax paper
- towels or small blankets
- pot lids or cookie sheets

Talk about why different surfaces produce different sounds when tapped. Explain that soft surfaces absorb sound like a sponge absorbs water. The harder the surface, the more quickly sound "bounces" off, which produces a louder sound.

Children may want to vote for their favorite sound.

Standing With Sticks

This activity is best for children who have been playing with rhythm sticks and following musical directions for at least several weeks.

Children should be standing in a circle, each child holding a pair of sticks. Put on some lively music with a regular beat; for example, a march. Encourage the children to copy your motions with the sticks—tapping, scraping, tapping toes with sticks (reach down and tap toes gently with the tops of your sticks), and so on.

Here's a more difficult variation to try: Tap your sticks while slowly squatting as low as possible, and then slowly come back up to a standing position.

Trot, Gallop, Freeze!

The children sit in a circle, each child holding a pair of sticks.

Put on some very lively music. (A good tune to use is the "William Tell Overture" by Rossini.) Tell the children that they will pretend to be horses— trotting (tapping gently), galloping (tapping the floor in a fast galloping rhythm), or "freezing" (stopping with their sticks "frozen"), following your lead.

While you play this game, emphasize the difference between the sedate, polite "trotting" and the exciting, racing "galloping." "Freeze" at unpredictable intervals for more fun.

The Cat and the Mouse

Sing the following song to the tune of "The Farmer in the Dell." While singing the first verse, tap the sticks on the floor, alternating left and right sticks, like a cat's paws walking.

> *There once was a cat,*
> *There once was a cat,*
> *Hi ho, the derry-o,*
> *There once was a cat.*

Sing the second verse in a high, squeaky voice while tapping the sticks together quickly and softly.

> *There once was a mouse,*
> *There once was a mouse,*
> *Hi ho, the derry-o,*
> *There once was a mouse.*

Tap on the floor while singing the next verse.

> *The cat chased the mouse,*
> *The cat chased the mouse,*
> *Hi ho, the derry-o,*
> *The cat chased the mouse.*

Sing and tap the next verse "mouse style" (in a high, squeaky voice while tapping the sticks together quickly and softly).

> *The mouse ran away,*
> *The mouse ran away,*
> *Hi ho, the derry-o,*
> *The mouse ran away.*

Tap on floor quickly while singing the next verse.

> *The cat ran faster,*
> *The cat ran faster,*
> *Hi ho, the derry-o,*
> *The cat ran faster.*

Sing and tap "mouse style," very fast.

> *The mouse got away,*
> *The mouse got away,*
> *Hi ho, the derry-o,*
> *The mouse got away!*

Put the sticks down and pretend to sleep.

> *The cat went to sleep,*
> *The cat went to sleep,*
> *Hi ho, the derry-o,*
> *The cat went to sleep.*

Hot Cross Buns

This song has a nice, clear rhythm for tapping. Sing, while tapping the sticks on each syllable:

> *Hot cross buns,*
> *Hot cross buns.*
> *One-a-penny, two-a-penny,*
> *Hot cross buns.*

Emphasize that the "one-a-penny, two-a-penny" beats are shorter and faster. (Musically, they are eighth notes as opposed to quarter notes.)

Then play it different ways—soft, loud, fast, slow, in a high voice, in a low voice, and so on. Ask the children for more ideas of different ways to play it.

Windshield Wipers

Note: This game requires a bit of extra "elbow room" between children.

This is a sound story in which the children follow your actions. Tell the children to pretend that their sticks are windshield wipers and that the floor is the car's front windows.

One day I went out for a drive. It was a beautiful sunny day (hold sticks still on the floor). *Then I noticed some clouds in the sky, and then some more clouds. Then it started to rain, so I turned on my windshield wipers* (swish sticks back and forth on the floor like windshield wipers).

After a while the rain stopped (hold sticks still). *Then it started again* (swish sticks). *Then it started to rain even harder, so I turned my wipers on high so they went faster* (swish sticks quickly). *Then the rain stopped again* (hold sticks still).

Continue for a few minutes.

You may want to let the children take turns leading this activity when they're familiar with it.

The Spider Went Over the Spider Web

Ask the children to sit cross-legged on the floor. Show them how to make their sticks do a "spider walk." Hold the sticks straight up and down and to the beat of the song "walk" them around on the floor, stiffly and lightly, to imitate a spider walking on its long, skinny legs.

Do the "spider walk" with the sticks while singing the following song to the tune of "The Bear Went Over the Mountain":

The spider went over the spider web,
The spider went over the spider web,
The spider went over the spider web,
To catch a little fly.

He caught a little fly.
He caught a little fly.
And he went back over the spider web,
He went back over the spider web,
He went back over the spider web,
And then he went to sleep.

When you "catch a fly," grab an imaginary fly with the ends of your sticks (using a chopstick motion, except using both hands). Then "spider walk" until the end of the song, when you put down the sticks and pretend to sleep.

Beethoven's 5th Symphony

This is a very easy and fun introduction to the music of Beethoven!

The children sit in a circle, each child holding a pair of sticks. Put on a recording of the opening of Beethoven's "5th Symphony." Tell the children that when they hear the four-note "da da da **da**" theme, they will tap their sticks firmly on the floor. When they hear the violins take over with high, light playing, they will scrape their sticks softly.

Play the song for about a minute, then repeat it from the beginning. Children love listening for the intense four-note theme and "accompanying" the music of Beethoven.

Jack and Jill

Why do children love the nursery rhyme, "Jack and Jill"? It's the falling down part, of course! While saying the rhyme, children have fun making the rhythm sticks "fall down" just like Jack and Jill did.

Chant the following rhyme while slowly tapping your sticks on the floor, alternating left and right:

> Jack and Jill went up the hill,
> To fetch a pail of water.
> Jack fell down, and broke his crown,
> And Jill came tumbling after.

On "Jack fell down," gently lie one of the sticks on the floor. Lie the other one down on "Jill came tumbling after."

"Painting" on the Floor

Put on a recording of soft, calm music. Encourage the children to pretend to paint on the floor with their rhythm sticks (one or both). You can suggest they try curly lines, straight lines, circles, triangles, flowers, a smiley face, or whatever they wish.

As a variation, go around the circle and ask each child to "paint" something and then have the group guess what it is.

Another variation is to put on a different style of music—maybe a marching band or some jazz—and ask the children to "paint" the way the new music sounds. Then you and the children can talk about the music and the paintings.

This is very neat way to paint—no mess!

Tap, Tap, Tap Your Boat

Tap to the beat while singing the following song to the tune of "Row, Row, Row Your Boat":

Tap, tap, tap your boat,
Gently down the stream.
Merrily, merrily, merrily, merrily,
Life is but a dream.

Additional verses:

Scrape, scrape, scrape your boat…

Pound, pound, pound your boat…

Hammer, hammer, hammer your boat…

Roll, roll, roll your boat…

Activities Using Shakers

There are many kinds of shakers (maracas). The traditional, drumstick-shaped ones are easy for children to handle. Plastic shakers are more durable than wood; however, you should check the condition of your shakers regularly because children can be very hard on them. Cracks can result in many little plastic beads rolling around on the floor!

I love shakers because of their incredible versatility. The quality of a shaker's sound changes when it is shaken vigorously or lightly, waved through the air, tapped on your palm, or rubbed gently on a shoulder or knee.

In addition, the drumstick shakers lend themselves to lots of dramatic play for preschoolers. They can be a vacuum cleaner, a broom, a baby, a toothbrush, a spoon, an animal, or almost anything children want them to be!

Young children love shakers—they're easy to play and make a loud and festive sound. Have fun with these activities!

Shakers Introduction

Shakers (maracas) are fun to play and make a terrific sound, and children absolutely love them!

Before putting the shakers into everybody's hands, it's a good idea to do an introductory lesson. Bring out *one* shaker and demonstrate how to shake it—*very gently*. Shakers are loud (that's why they're fun, of course!), and a room full of shakers played by enthusiastic preschoolers can be deafening. A little shaking goes a long way!

Use a short movement of the wrist to shake the shaker and talk about how you're moving just your wrist. Ask the children to copy your movement, while holding their arms still. Explain that this is a "special trick" to make the shakers sound really great. Everyone loves a special trick!

Pass the shaker around the circle and let each child practice playing the shaker with correct form. Be sure to notice how well they're doing the special trick!

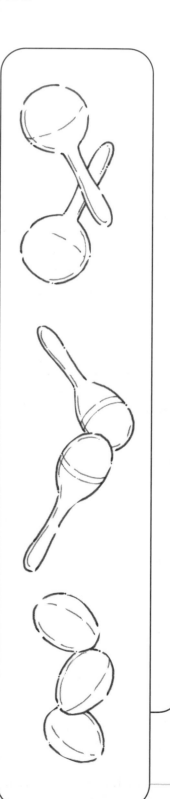

Different Ways to Play Shakers

Put on a tape of instrumental music with a steady beat. Encourage the children to copy you as you play the shaker in different ways. Here are some ideas:

- tap the shaker into the palm of your other hand
- hold the shaker upside down and shake
- "rub" the shaker on the floor
- shake high in the air
- rub the shaker on your arm
- hold the shaker horizontally in both hands and shake
- shake "out and in"—hold your arm straight out in front, and then bring it back in (to the beat)
- make circles in the air with the shaker
- shake up and down
- shake side to side
- shake the shaker behind your back
- rub the shaker on your tummy
- gently tap the shaker on your shoe
- "vacuum" the floor in front of you with the shaker
- "sweep" the floor, using the shaker like a broom
- twirl the shaker, using both hands
- rub the shaker on your shoulder

Going to Kentucky

This traditional song is lots of fun to sing and dance to while shaking shakers. The children should be standing in a circle, each child holding a shaker. Encourage the children to shake to the beat while swaying a bit from side to side.

> *I was going to Kentucky, going to the fair,*
> *To see the señorita with the flowers in her hair.*
> *Oh, shake it, shake it, shake it,*
> *Shake it if you can,*
> *Shake it like a milkshake,* (shake hard)
> *And do the best you can.*

(continued on next page)

Oh, wobble to the bottom, (shake while shimmying down to a squatting position)
Wobble to the top. (shake while standing up and raising the shaker high)
And turn around and turn around until you make a stop! (turn around—not too fast—and freeze on the word "stop")

Waltz of the Flowers

Tell the children they are going to pretend that the shakers are flowers.

For this activity, put on a recording of the "Waltz of the Flowers" from the *Nutcracker Suite* by Tchaikovsky. Tell a little about the background of this piece—that Tchaikovsky wrote this music about magic flowers that come to life and dance.

Children can copy your motions or make up some of their own. Here are some ideas for "dance moves" for your shakers:

- hold the handle like a "stem" and make the shaker hop and dance lightly on the floor
- hold the handle and slowly raise the shaker high above your head, then slowly lower it again
- hold the handle and do slow, graceful figure eights in the air
- lift the shaker shoulder-high to the left, then sway it to the right
- make little circles in the air
- hold the shaker upside down and make little circles
- hold the shaker like a stem and "kick" with the stem

Wake Up, Groundhog!

This very silly activity is perfect for Groundhog Day, but children want to play it all year round!

Children should be sitting in a circle, each child holding a shaker. Choose one child to be the "groundhog." The groundhog sits in the middle of the circle, hiding under a small blanket (this represents the groundhog's hole).

The children shake their shakers softly to the beat and sing the following song to the tune of "Good Night, Ladies":

> *Wake up, groundhog,*
> *Wake up, groundhog.*
> *Wake up, groundhog,*
> *It's Groundhog Day today!*

At the end of the song, everyone shouts, "Wake up, groundhog!" and shakes very loudly. Then the groundhog can pop out from under the blanket!

Experiments With Shakers

Introduce this activity by asking the children how they think shakers make a sound. Tell them that they're going to explore how different things can make different sounds when shaken in containers.

Use a clean, empty, plastic peanut butter jar with a top for the container. Bring out various items to fill the jar, and encourage the children to try shaking them in the container. (Pass each new "invention" around the circle for everyone to try.) Some ideas for materials to use include:

- dried beans
- rice
- dry cereal such as oat rings
- cotton balls
- jingle bells
- pennies
- small plastic building bricks

Ask the children to describe the sounds they hear. Which are loudest? Softest? Nicest? Most interesting?

They may want to vote on their favorite sound. Also, they may have ideas for other materials to use. This could turn into an ongoing project!

SAFETY NOTE: If children are still putting things into their mouths, supervise this activity very closely.

This Is the Way We Clean the House

In improvising with children over the years, I've found that shakers seem to remind children of several household chores! (So I made up a song about it.)

Sing the following song to the tune of "Here We Go 'Round the Mulberry Bush":

> *This is the way we dust the ceiling,* (hold shaker up like a feather duster and
> pretend to dust the ceiling)
> *Dust the ceiling, dust the ceiling.*
> *This is the way we dust the ceiling,*
> *So early in the morning.*

Additional verses:

> *This is the way we sweep the floor…*(sweep shaker like a broom on the floor)
>
> *This is the way we scrub the floor…*(hold the wide part of the shaker like a sponge
> and gently rub the floor)
>
> *This is the way we vacuum the floor…*(hold the handle of the shaker and "vacuum")
>
> *This is the way we water the plants…*(hold the wide part of the shaker, pretend
> the handle is a spout, and pretend to
> water plants)

Children may have even more ideas for cleaning the house with the shakers!

Wind Song

Sing the following song to the tune of "London Bridge Is Falling Down." While singing, gently sway the shaker from side to side.

> *Wind can be a gentle breeze,*
> *Gentle breeze, gentle breeze.*
> *Wind can be a gentle breeze,*
> *In the summer.*

Additional verses:

> *Wind can make the leaves fall down,*   (make falling motion with shaker)
> *Leaves fall down, leaves fall down.*
> *Wind can make the leaves fall down,*
> *In the fall.*

> *Wind can be an icy blast,*   (hold shaker tightly and "shiver")
> *Icy blast, icy blast.*
> *Wind can be an icy blast,*
> *In the winter.*

> *Wind can help you fly a kite,*   (sway shaker high above head like a kite)
> *Fly a kite, fly a kite.*
> *Wind can help you fly a kite,*
> *In the springtime.*
> > by Abigail Flesch Connors

Ocean Waves

In this game you can imagine you're at the beach, listening to the waves. Show the children how to make the sound of the waves by holding their shaker and gently rolling it out and back in on the floor in front of them.

Start with "low tide" and make small, gentle waves. Let the tide get higher and make stronger and louder waves. For giant waves at high tide, lift the shaker off the floor and roll in the air with a large cranking motion before landing (not too hard!) on the floor and subsiding.

Go through the sequence backwards, ending back at low tide and soft, gentle waves.

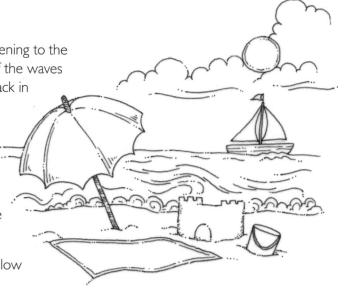

Stir Up My Soup

Tell the children that their shakers will become "spoons" for this song as they stir imaginary pots of soup.

Sing the following song to the tune of "My Bonnie Lies Over the Ocean":

First put in some carrots and celery,
Some chicken and noodles and peas.
But please don't put in too much pepper,
'Cause pepper will make you sneeze. AH-CHOO!

Stir up, stir up,
Oh, stir up my soup for me, for me.
Stir up, stir up,
Oh, stir up my soup for me.

When children know this song well, ask them for ideas for other kinds of food to put in the soup—the sillier the better! Ask for four ideas per verse, and keep the "peas" in to rhyme with "sneeze."

For example:

First put in some spaghetti and candy,
Some ice cream and hot dogs and peas...

Children find this activity hilarious!

Shake It High and Shake It Low

Sing the following song to the tune of "London Bridge Is Falling Down":

Shake your shaker in the air,	(shake shaker high above head)
Shake it here, shake it there.	(shake left, then right)
Shake your shaker in the air,	(shake shaker high above head)
Shake your shaker.	

Shake it high and shake it low,	(shake high in air, then low near the ground)
Shake it yes, shake it no.	(shake up and down while nodding, side to side while shaking head)
Shake it high and shake it low,	(hold shaker high and low)
Shake your shaker.	(shake strongly on each syllable)
Shake it up and shake it down,	(shake shaker high, then low)
Rub your shaker on the ground.	(gently rub shaker on the floor in front of you)
Shake it up and shake it down,	(shake shaker high, then low)
Shake your shaker.	
Shake it near and shake it far,	(shake shaker close to body, then out at arm's length)
Drive your shaker like a car.	(hold shaker with both hands horizontally and "drive" like a steering wheel)
Shake it near and shake it far,	(shake shaker close to body, then out at arm's length)
Shake your shaker.	
Shake it fast and shake it slow,	(shake fast, then very slow)
Shake it stop, shake it go.	(freeze on the word "stop;" continue on the word "go")
Shake it fast and shake it slow,	(shake fast, then very slow)
Shake your shaker.	

You can use this activity to begin a discussion or lesson on opposites. Ask the children if they remember some of the pairs of opposites in the song. "What are some more pairs of opposites you could act out with the shakers?"

Shaker Square Dance

Here's a great way to enjoy all the boisterous fun of a square dance even if you don't have enough room for the real kind.

Put on some square dance music. If possible, it should be instrumental—words can be distracting and you want the children to listen to your directions.

The children should be sitting in a circle, each child holding a shaker. Ask the children to hold their shakers by the handle so that the shakers are "standing" on the floor in front of them. As the music begins, call out the following "steps" for the children to perform with the shakers.

1. Bow to your "partner" on one side.
2. Bow to your "partner" on the other side.
3. Take four steps forward, four steps back (repeat).
4. Tip shaker from side to side.
5. Step in a circle.
6. Jump high (eight times).
7. "Kick" with your shaker (eight times).
8. Spin your shaker.
9. Turn somersaults.
10. Have the shaker dance on its "head."
11. Roll on its side.
12. Bow to "partners" again and the dance is done!

Digging Up a Hole

In this activity, the versatile shaker portrays a shovel, a rake, the sun, a watering can, and a plant!

Sing the following song to the tune of the "Dinah, Won't You Blow?" section of "I've Been Working on the Railroad":

> *Digging up a hole, digging up a hole,*
> (hold shaker like a shovel and "dig")
> *Digging up a hole to-da-a-ay.*
> *Digging up a hole, digging up a hole,*
> *Digging up a hole today!*

(Before the next verse, pretend to drop a seed in the hole.)

Additional verses:

> *Raking up the dirt…*(pretend to rake with shaker)

> *Sun is gonna shine…*(shake shaker high in the air, swaying)

> *Watering the plant…*(hold the round part of the shaker and "water" through the handle)

> *Plant is gonna grow…*(hold shaker straight up on ground and lift it slowly as if it's "growing")

Ask the children for suggestions for what kind of plant they would like to grow—a flower? A vegetable?

Use this activity as part of a unit on gardening, or after reading a story about planting.

Little Baby

Preschoolers are fascinated with babies, and this activity is a great opportunity to talk about babies and what they like to do.

Sing the following song to the tune of "London Bridge Is Falling Down":

> *Little baby go to sleep,*
> *Go to sleep, go to sleep.*
> *Little baby go to sleep,*
> *Little baby.* (rock shaker in
>   arms like a baby)

Additional verses:

> *Little baby start to crawl…*(hold shaker horizontally
>   on floor and make it "crawl")

> *Little baby start to walk…*(hold shaker upright on floor and make it "walk")

> *Little baby start to run…*(make the shaker "run" while you sing this verse very fast)

> *Little baby start to jump…* (make shaker "jump" on floor)

> *Little baby go to sleep…* (after all that activity, baby needs to take another nap!)

Ask the children what else the baby might like to do. Climb? Roll around? Maybe play peek-a-boo!

The Animals in the Jungle

Shakers are such incredibly versatile instruments. With their distinctive shape and easy-to-maneuver usability, they can be anything you want them to be—all you need is a little imagination. In this activity the shakers become jungle animals!

Sing the following song to the tune of "The Wheels on the Bus":

> *The snake in the jungle goes wiggle, wiggle, wiggle,* (hold shaker flat on floor and wiggle it around)
>
> *Wiggle, wiggle, wiggle,*
> *Wiggle, wiggle, wiggle.*
> *The snake in the jungle goes wiggle, wiggle, wiggle,*
> *All through the jungle.*

Additional verses:

> *The elephant in the jungle has a great big trunk…*(hold shaker from nose like a trunk and sway from side to side)
>
> *The monkey in the jungle goes climb, climb, climb…*(hold shaker upright and make it climb up an imaginary tree)
>
> *The turtle in the jungle has a hard, hard shell…*("knock" on head of shaker with knuckles)

The leopard in the jungle has spots, spots, spots…(point to your "spots"
with the shaker)

The frog in the jungle goes jump, jump, jump…(make shaker jump on floor)

The bird in the jungle goes fly, fly, fly…(make shaker fly through the air)

This is a good tie-in activity for a unit on jungle animals, or you can sing this song after reading a story about the jungle.

Where Is Shaker?

Put the shaker behind your back. Ask the children, "Where is Shaker? He's behind my back! But he'll come out to do some tricks."

Sing the following song to the tune of "Where Is Thumbkin?":

Where is Shaker? Where is Shaker? (begin with the shaker held behind your back)
Here I am! Here I am! (bring the shaker out and shake it)
How are you today, friend? Very well, I thank you. (pretend to talk to the shaker and
have it answer you)
Run away, run away. (hide the shaker behind your back again)

Before singing the next verse, explain that when Shaker comes out this time, instead of talking, he's going to do something different. First, he'll roll on the floor.

Where is Shaker? Where is Shaker?
Here I am! Here I am!
Rolling on the floor, rolling on the floor. (roll shaker on the floor)
Run away, run away.

Additional verses (same as above except line 3):

Tapping on your hand, tapping on your hand… (tap shaker on palm of
opposite hand)

Shaking on your tummy, shaking on your tummy… (roll shaker gently on
your tummy)

Jumping up and down, jumping up and down… (hold shaker upright and make
it "jump" on the floor)

Ask children for their ideas for more "tricks" for Shaker to do when he comes out.

Shaker Parade

This is a good activity when you feel like having a parade, but you're cramped for space. This is a fun activity for Memorial Day, St. Patrick's Day, or the Fourth of July.

Put on some marching music—any John Phillip Sousa march is great, or "McNamara's Band" for St. Patrick's Day. Children should be sitting in a circle, each child holding a shaker. Explain that the shakers are going to "march" as in a parade. (To "march" your shaker, hold it upright and make it step very sharply and precisely to the beat.) Try the following:

- march out toward the middle of the circle, then back in
- march to one side, then march to the other side
- march up and down your legs
- march up your arm, all the way to the top of your head, and back down the other arm
- march up a pretend hill, then march back down
- march the shaker on its head (hold shaker upside down)
- end with a big loud shake!

Who Will Help Me?
(The Little Red Hen)

This activity is based on the story "The Little Red Hen." If you play this with the children after reading the story, they will enjoy remembering the tasks the Little Red Hen had to accomplish in order to make bread from a few grains of wheat. Remembering the tasks in the correct order is a fun challenge! The physical movements and sound texture help to reinforce the story and make it more meaningful.

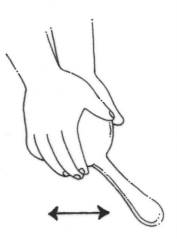

Sing the following song to the tune of "Here We Go 'Round the Mulberry Bush":

Who will help me water the wheat, (hold the round part of the
shaker and pour as if from a
watering can)
Water the wheat, water the wheat?
Who will help me water the wheat,
So early in the morning?

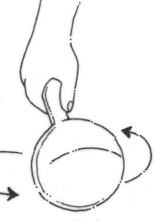

Additional verses:

Who will help me cut the wheat… (hold the round part of the shaker with both hands and "cut" as if with a knife)

Who will help me take the wheat… (push shaker on the ground like a wheelbarrow)

Who will help me bake the bread… (hold shaker like a spoon and "stir" batter)

Who will help me eat the bread… (hold shaker like a piece of bread and pretend to eat it)

Shakers Count to Ten

This is a chant, similar to "One, Two, Buckle My Shoe." You may want to ask the children to come up with other rhymes that can be performed with the shakers—for example, "One, two, shake on something blue." Have fun!

One, two, shake it on your shoe, (roll shaker gently on your shoe)
Three, four, shake it on the floor, (roll shaker gently on the floor)
Five, six, stir and mix, (holding shaker upside down like a spoon, pretend to stir)

Seven, eight, stand up straight, (hold shaker in "standing" position on floor)
Nine, ten, wave to all your friends! (wave shaker in the air)

For extra fun, when all the children know this rhyme well, you can try performing it slow, at regular speed, fast, and then *very* fast!

Teddy Bear Shakers

Everyone loves teddy bears! Preschoolers also love the fun of suddenly going very fast, which this activity allows them to do. They'll want to sing this one over and over again. Sing the first two lines fairly slowly to the tune of "Twinkle, Twinkle, Little Star":

Teddy bears, teddy bears, (hold shaker in "standing" position on floor, gently "jumping" them to the beat)

Like to sit in teddy chairs. (have shaker "sit" in opposite hand)
Then—they—like—to— (sing slowly on one note)
Runaroundrunaroundrunaroundrunar (sing very fast, with shaker in "standing"
oundRUN! position running fast in a circle)

Be sure to say, "And down," or some other signal so the children stop their shakers from "running" and put them down.

Additional verses:

Teddy bears, teddy bears,
Like to climb up teddy stairs… (have the shaker walk up imaginary stairs)

Teddy bears, teddy bears,
Like to brush their teddy hair… (hold shaker in "standing" position, pretend to brush its hair)

If you're having a "Teddy Bear Day," you can do this activity with real teddy bears!

I'm a Little Raindrop

Here's a fun little song for a rainy day.

Standing, hold your shaker so that it is hanging "upside down" above your head. Sing the following song to the tune of "I'm a Little Teapot":

> *I'm a little raindrop in the sky,*
> *While I am up here, you're nice and dry.*
> *When the time is right I get all set,* (wiggle your shaker gently)
> *I fall down and you get wet!* (bring your shaker down with a fast motion)

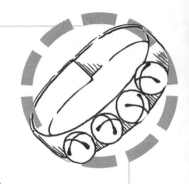

Activities Using Jingle Bells

Jingle bells aren't just for winter! They're lots of fun anytime—nothing else has quite the same happy sound.

Jingle bells are related to shaker-type instruments in that they both make sound by rattling small objects in a container. The only difference is that the bells are made entirely of metal rather than wood or plastic, so they have a brighter, sharper sound.

I like to attach jingle bells to bracelets using Velcro so that for some activities, the children have the option of wearing the bells on their wrists or ankles. These are easy for children to use—which means easy for you, too—and they are quite durable. In addition, activities in which bells are worn on wrists or ankles will emphasize and reinforce learning about parts of the body and movement awareness. Children are fascinated with pulling off the Velcro and attaching it again, so you may want to let them play with this for a minute or two so they get it out of their systems before you start an activity!

You can also purchase bells on plastic bracelets, or make bell bracelets yourself (or as a class project) by weaving pipe cleaners through the jingle bells.

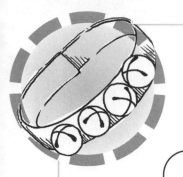

Jingle Bells Introduction

Introduce the jingle bells by bringing out one bell bracelet and showing the children how they will be playing it most of the time—holding it (not wearing it) and shaking it gently.

You may want to talk about what it's made of and compare it to the other instruments the children have played. Ask them questions. "What were the rhythm sticks made of?" "What about the shakers?" "How does the metal cause the bells to have a different sound?" "How do the bells actually make their sound?" "What else is made of metal?"

Pass the bell bracelet around the circle, allowing each child a turn to shake it and look it over.

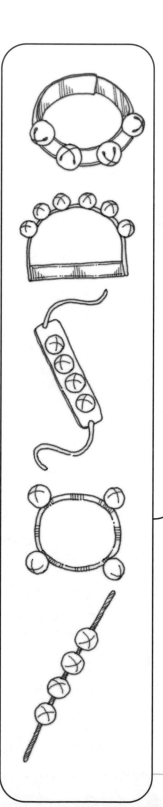

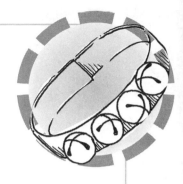

Different Ways to Play Bells

Put on a tape of instrumental music with a moderately fast, steady beat. Encourage the children to copy your motions as you play the bells in different ways. Here are some ideas you can try:

- shake bells up and down
- shake bells side to side
- make a circle in the air with the bells
- tap the floor gently
- tap your shoes gently
- tap the palm of your other hand, very gently
- shake bells behind your back
- rub your tummy with the bells
- shake bells "out and in"—hold them out at arm's length and bring them back in, to the beat of the music
- hold bells enclosed in both hands and shake
- twirl bells on pointer finger

Jingle Bells

It seems that every time preschoolers see bells, no matter what the season, they start to sing "Jingle Bells!" So, I suggest that the children sing and jingle together!

Jingle bells, jingle bells, jingle all the way,
Oh, what fun it is to ride in a one-horse open sleigh—Hey!
Jingle bells, jingle bells, jingle all the way,
Oh, what fun it is to ride in a one-horse open sleigh!

Sometimes it's fun (particularly during the actual holiday season) to arrange the children on the floor as if they're really riding in a sleigh. They can jostle around as if it's a bumpy ride.

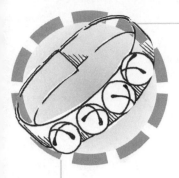

Little Jingle Mouse

Sing the following song to the tune of "Going to Kentucky" (this tune is also "99 Bottles of Pop on the Wall"):

I heard a little jingle,   (jingle bells softly)
Right inside my house.
It sounded like the jingle
Of a little jingle mouse.
He jingled to the ceiling,   (jingle bells high over head)
He jingled to the floor,   (jingle bells on floor)
He jingled till he fell asleep,   (hold jingle bells in arms like a baby)
And he began to snore…
(snooore, snoore, snooore)   (jingle bells very gently while doing a tiny,
    squeaky snore)

I heard a great big jingle,   (jingle bells loudly)
Right outside my door,
It sounded like the jingle
Of a jingle dinosaur.
He jingled to the ceiling,   (jingle bells high over head)
He jingled to the floor,   (jingle bells on floor)
He jingled till he fell asleep,   (hold jingle bells in arms like a baby)
And he began to snore…
(snooore, snoore, snooore)   (jingle bells and snore very loudly)

We're Passing Around the Bells

Sing the following song to the tune of "The Farmer in the Dell":

We're passing around the bells,
We're passing around the bells,
Hi-ho, the derry-o,
We're passing around the bells.

The children sit in a circle with one child in the middle. The child in the middle keeps his eyes closed while the group sings the song and passes around one bell bracelet. At the end of the song, whoever has the bells holds them behind her back. The rest of the

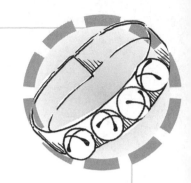

children also put their hands behind their backs. Ask the child in the middle to open his eyes and guess who has the bells. (You may want to give the child three tries.) The child holding the bells is the next one to be in the middle.

Twinkle, Twinkle, Little Star

If twinkling stars made sounds, it would probably sound like jingle bells!

Twinkle, twinkle, little star,	(jingle bells softly)
How I wonder what you are.	
Up above the world so high,	(hold bells up high, "in the sky")
Like a diamond in the sky,	
Twinkle, twinkle, little star,	(bring bells back down and jingle softly)
How I wonder what you are.	

Try singing and jingling the song in different ways: very, very softly (in a whisper), very slowly, very fast, and so on.

Bells or Shaker?

This is an easy game to encourage the children to focus on careful listening.

Ask the children to sit in a circle. The teacher has a bell bracelet and a shaker. Going around the circle, give each child a turn.

The child whose turn it is faces away from the circle with her eyes closed. Play either the bells or the shaker for a few moments. Then ask the child which instrument she heard. Be sure to notice the children's excellent listening!

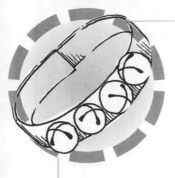

Bells in Socks

This is a sound-exploration experiment. Bring out a bell bracelet and jingle it. Then bring out a thick sock. Ask the children, "What would it sound like if you put the bells in the sock and then jingled it? Do you think it would sound softer? Louder? The same?" Then try it (or let a child try it) and see what happens.

Try other sound experiments with the bells. Ask, "What would it sound like if you held the bells very tightly in both hands and then shook them?" Then try it.

Ask the children, "What if you put the bells in an empty coffee can, put the lid on, and shook it? Would it sound louder or softer than playing the bells the regular way?" Put the bells into a coffee can and try it.

Encourage the children to use their imaginations to think of other ways to change the sound of the bells.

Bells on Ankles

Ask the children to stand in a circle.

Put on some lively music with a steady beat. Ask the children to attach the bells around their ankles, helping those who need it.

See how many moves you and the children can come up with to make music with bells on your ankles. Here are some ideas to get you started:

- stamp feet
- kick
- tap toes
- hop on belled foot
- jump with both feet
- wiggle belled foot
- run in place
- tiptoe in place

As a variation, you can play this game sitting down, with feet out in front of you.

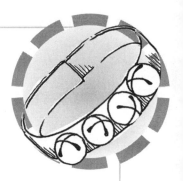

Freeze Dance With Bells

Bells add an extra (loud) dimension to the freeze dance game. Ask the children to attach bells around their wrists. Then put on some fun dance music.

Everyone dances until you stop the music. When the music stops, the children "freeze" in place like statues. When you restart the music, everyone dances again. Continue for a few minutes.

The bells make the game noisier (which is always fun) and also make "freezing" more of a challenge, because their jingling will give them away if they continue moving!

Jingle at the Window

Any song with the word "jingle" in the title is a natural for playing with jingle bells!

Children stand in a circle, holding bells, and sing the following song:

> *Pass one window, ti-de-o,*   (take a very small step in toward the center of the circle and jingle three times on "ti-de-o")
> *Pass two windows, ti-de-o,*   (take a small step in, three jingles on "ti-de-o")
> *Pass three windows, ti-de-o,*   (take a small step in, three jingles on "ti-de-o")
> *Jingle at the window, ti-de-o.*   (raise bells high in air and jingle)
>
> *Jingle, jingle, jingle, jo,*   (jingle while turning around)
> *Jingle at the window, ti-de-o.*   (raise bells high in air and jingle)

Sing the song again, but this time take steps backwards to return to the original circle.

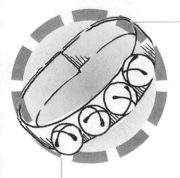

Hickory Dickory Dock

The pitter-patter of little mouse feet is musically portrayed by jingle bells in this version of the nursery rhyme.

Children sit in a circle, each holding a bell bracelet. Sing the following song:

Hickory, dickory, dock! (hold left hand up, palm facing out, to be the clock)
The mouse ran up the clock, (jingle bells as you make them "run up the clock")
The clock struck one, (make a "1" with the pointer finger of your left hand)
The mouse ran down, (run down the "clock" with the bells in your right hand)
Hickory, dickory, dock. (jingle bells three times, on **hick**ory **dick**ory **dock)**

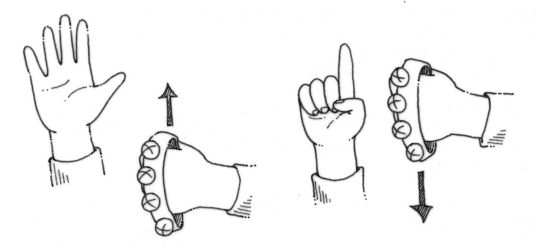

Hold up two fingers of your left hand (the "clock") and sing:

Hickory, dickory, dock!
The mouse ran up the clock,
The clock struck two,
The mouse sneezed "AH-CHOO!" ("sneeze" loudly and jingle your bells)
Hickory, dickory, dock!

Hold up three fingers of your left hand and sing:

Hickory, dickory, dock!
The mouse ran up the clock,
The clock struck three,
The mouse said, "Wheee!"   (sing "Wheee!" in a high squeaky voice while
Hickory, dickory, dock!   making the bells "slide" down the clock)

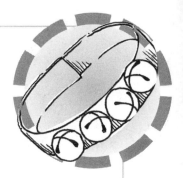

Circus Tricks With Bells

It's circus time! Put on some lively music. "The Entry of the Gladiators" (a traditional circus theme composed by Julius Fucik*) is fun if it's available, but any exciting music will work.

Try these amazing feats:

Juggling—(Don't worry, this is not really juggling!) Each child has one bell bracelet. With their hands close together, they gently toss the bells from one hand to the other and back. Tell them to gradually increase the distance between their hands a bit. If they want to get fancy, they can try tossing the bells up (gently, maybe six or eight inches high) and catching them with the other hand.

Spinning Plates—This is the bells version of the trick where people spin plates on long sticks. Spin the bell bracelet on your pointer finger. After a while, try moving your hand up and down while spinning the bells on your finger. Try moving your hand out to arm's length and back while continuing to spin the bells.

Bells Tightrope Challenge—This is tricky, but fun even when you mess up. Put a long strip of masking tape on the floor to be the tightrope. Here's the hard part: the children put their bell bracelet on top of their heads and try to walk along the tightrope without the bells falling off. Be sure each child has a turn.

*This recording is found on *25 Thunderous Classics*, Vox (Classical), 2000 and *Preschool Playtime Band*, Kimbo, 1987.

Jingle Around the Rosie

Here are two ways to play "Ring Around the Rosie" with jingle bells.

Play "Ring Around the Rosie" the traditional way, except that each child is wearing a bell bracelet. When they "all fall down," it will be extra noisy and extra fun!

Another way to play is for the children to sit in a circle holding their bell bracelets. While singing the song, the children can move the bells in front of them in a horizontal circle (parallel to the floor), a few inches above the ground. At the end of the song, the children can let the bells drop to the floor.

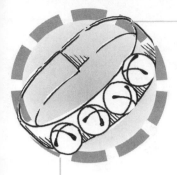

Frère Jacques

Here are two ways to use this traditional tune with jingle bells.

One way is for the children to sit in a circle, each holding a jingle bell bracelet. The children pretend to sleep (eyes closed, head on folded hands) and sing the first two lines:

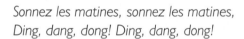

> *Frère Jacques, Frère Jacques,*
> *Dormez-vous? Dormez-vous?*

Then they "wake up" and jingle their bells as they sing the next two lines:

> *Sonnez les matines, sonnez les matines,*
> *Ding, dang, dong! Ding, dang, dong!*

(You may prefer the English version below.)

> *Are you sleeping, are you sleeping,*
> *Brother John, Brother John?*
> *Morning bells are ringing,*
> *Morning bells are ringing,*
> *Ding, dang, dong! Ding, dang, dong!*

Another way to use this tune is to sing the following song to the tune of "Frère Jacques":

> *Can you jingle, can you jingle*
> *On your toes? On your toes?*
> *Yes, we can jingle, yes, we can jingle*
> *On our toes, on our toes!*

Continue with as many verses as you like, jingling your bells on your knees, elbows, shoulders, tummy, the floor, and so on.

All About Colors

Bells are not essential to this activity, but they add a nice musical texture. The verses don't have to be performed in this order—let the children call out the colors they want to sing about.

Ask the children to attach the bell bracelets around their wrists.

Sing the following song to the tune of "Skip to My Lou":

Red, red is the color of an apple,
Let's reach up and pick an apple,   ("reach" up to pick an
                                                      apple from a tree)

Pick an apple, pick an apple,
Red is the color of an apple.

Green, green is the color of a frog,
Let's all hop just like a frog,   (squat on the floor and hop)
Hop like a frog, hop like a frog,
Green is the color of a frog.

Blue, blue is the color of the ocean,
Let's all swim in the big blue ocean,   ("swim" with arms)
Swim in the ocean, swim in the ocean,
Blue is the color of the ocean.

Yellow, yellow is the color of flowers,
Let's bend down and pick some flowers,   (pick "flowers" from floor)
Pick some flowers, pick some flowers,
Yellow is the color of flowers.

Orange, orange is the color of juice,
Let's all drink a cup of juice,   (pretend to drink from a cup)
Drink some juice, drink some juice,
Orange is the color of juice.

Purple, purple is the color of grapes,
Let's all eat some purple grapes,   (pretend to pick grapes from a bunch
                                                      and eat them)

Eat some grapes, eat some grapes,
Purple is the color of grapes.

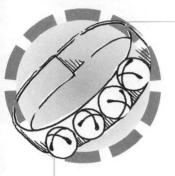

Black, black is the color of the night,
Let's all go to sleep at night, (pretend to sleep on folded hands, singing very
softly and slowly like a lullaby)
Go to sleep, go to sleep,
Black is the color of the night.

Nice and Warm

This is a fun activity for the winter months when "bundling up" is important.

Sing the following song to the tune of "London Bridge Is Falling Down":

Wear a hat upon your head, (gently roll bells on top of head)
On your head, on your head,
Wear a hat upon your head,
So you'll stay nice and warm.

Wear a scarf around your neck, (gently jingle bells next to your neck)
Around your neck, around your neck,
Wear a scarf around your neck,
So you'll stay nice and warm.

Wear some mittens on your hands, (gently roll bells on your hand)
On your hands, on your hands,
Wear some mittens on your hands,
So you'll stay nice and warm.

Wear some boots upon your feet, (gently jingle bells on your feet)
On your feet, on your feet,
Wear some boots upon your feet,
So you'll stay nice and warm.

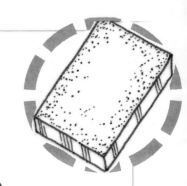

Activities Using Sand Blocks

Sand blocks are rectangles of fine-grained sandpaper attached to blocks of wood. They are available both with and without small wooden handles on the back. I use the kind with handles because they are much easier for little hands to play.

Sand blocks are very popular with young children, and understandably so! The "shuff-shuff" sound of sand blocks being lightly scraped is so intriguing—children's faces light up as soon as they hear it. Sand blocks also can be clapped for an intensely sharp, loud sound. Explore all the options for making noise with these interesting instruments—try hitting the sides of the blocks together, or put one on the floor and hit it with the other one. Let the children discover other ways to play, too.

One of the best things about sand blocks is that, when scraped, they sound remarkably like the "chugga-chugga, chugga-chugga" of a choo-choo train. This opens up many fun opportunities for play!

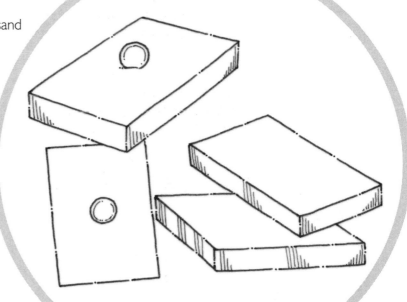

Sand Blocks Introduction

Bring out one pair of sand blocks and show the children how to scrape them together in a back-and-forth motion to make a wonderful "shuff-shuff" sound. Explain that the blocks also can be clapped together, but that they won't be doing that very often because it's very, **very** loud. Demonstrate.

Show the children the sandpaper on the blocks and explain how that makes the scraping sound. Ask, "Does anyone know what sandpaper is usually used for?"

Remind the children not to put the sand blocks near their faces. Pass the sand blocks around the circle and allow each child a turn to try them out.

The Train Is Coming

The scraping sound of sand blocks always reminds me of a train. Children love trains, and they will enjoy playing "train games" using sand blocks. Here is an easy one to try.

Chant "The train is com-ing" very slowly and softly as you scrape the blocks slowly and softly. (Explain that at first the train is heard from far away.)

Then, the train gets closer. Chant and scrape a bit faster.

Keep picking up the pace (and the volume) as the train comes closer and closer.

End with "Now the train is here!" and clap blocks loudly.

Different Ways to Play Sand Blocks

Play moderately lively music with a steady beat.

Children should be sitting in a circle, each with a pair of sand blocks. Ask the children to copy your motions as you play the sand blocks in different ways. Here are some suggestions to get you started:

- scrape blocks back and forth
- scrape in an up-and-down motion
- clap blocks together
- clap sides of blocks together
- hold blocks "backwards" and tap handles together
- put one block on floor and tap with other block
- tap ends of blocks together
- tap ends of blocks on the floor
- scrape very softly
- "clap" very softly
- tap ends of blocks on shoes

Ask children for their ideas, too!

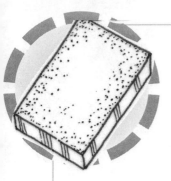

The Train Is Going Up the Hill

Sing the following song to the tune of "Here We Go 'Round the Mulberry Bush". While singing, the children scrape their sand blocks while slowly raising them high above their heads.

The train is going up the hill,
Up the hill, up the hill.
The train is going up the hill,
So early in the morning.

Additional verses:

The train is going down the hill… (scrape blocks while lowering them to the floor)

The train is going around the lake… (scrape blocks while moving them around an imaginary lake)

The train has hit a little bump… (on the word "bump," clap blocks together)

Just for fun, repeat the whole sequence while going very fast. Children love this!

Engine, Engine, Number Nine

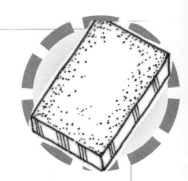

This old favorite is even more fun to sing when using sand blocks (which add the "choo-choo" sound).

Ask four or five children at a time to form a train in the middle of the circle. They chug around in the circle while the others scrape their sand blocks and chant or sing:

> *Engine, engine, number nine,*
> *Going down Chicago line,*
> *If the train goes off the track,*
> *Do you want your money back?*

On the words "off the track," the children in the "train" fall down. On the word "back," children with sand blocks clap them together.

The Sand Blocks Went to a Party

Children should be sitting in a circle, each holding sand blocks. The children scrape their sand blocks to the beat as they sing the following song to the tune of "The Bear Went Over the Mountain":

> *The sand blocks went to a party,*
> *The sand blocks went to a party,*
> *The sand blocks went to a party,*
> *And danced a little dance.*

After this verse, chant "step, step, cha-cha-cha; step, step, cha-cha-cha" while making the sand blocks "step" on the floor on "step, step" and scrape on "cha-cha-cha."

Additional verses:

> *The sand blocks went to a party… and ate a little food.*

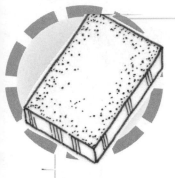

After this verse, chant "piz-za and birthday cake; piz-za and birthday cake" while making the sand blocks "step" on floor on "piz-za" and scrape on "birthday cake."

The sand blocks went to a party… and played a little game.

After this verse, chant "they played Si-mon-Says; they played Si-mon-Says" while making the sand blocks "step" on floor on "they played" and scrape on "Si-mon-Says."

When the children are familiar with this activity, ask them to come up with ideas for other things to eat at the party and other games to play.

Happy Birthday Cha-Cha-Cha

This is a great way to celebrate a child's birthday. It can also be used to celebrate famous birthdays such as George Washington's. (One child can pretend to be George Washington and everyone can sing, "Happy birthday, dear George Washington.")

The birthday child stands at the front of the room, facing the class. The other children stand facing the child, holding sand blocks. They are the "candles" on a giant imaginary birthday cake. Sing:

> *Happy birthday to you, cha-cha-cha,*
> *Happy birthday to you, cha-cha-cha,*
> *Happy birthday, dear _____, cha-cha-cha,*
> *Happy birthday to you, cha-cha-cha!*

On "cha-cha-cha," children scrape the sand blocks. At the end of the song, the birthday child "blows out the candles" and all the children (gently) fall to the floor. (If space is tight, just have the children squat down.)

In the Middle of the Night

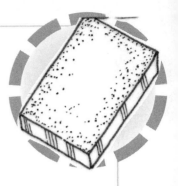

Sand blocks can be used to imitate a variety of sounds associated with nighttime. Children enjoy this opportunity to discuss the sometimes strange or scary noises they hear at night.

Sing the following song to the tune of "London Bridge Is Falling Down":

> *In the middle of the night,*
> *I hear the wind, I hear the wind,*   (scrape sand blocks softly to imitate the sound of wind blowing)
> *In the middle of the night,*
> *I hear the wind.*
> *In the middle of the night,*
> *I hear footsteps, I hear footsteps,*   ("step" with blocks on the floor)
> *In the middle of the night,*
> *I hear footsteps.*

Additional verses:

> *In the middle of the night,*
> *I hear a door,…*   (open and shut blocks, held like a book)

> *In the middle of the night,*
> *I hear rain,…*   (scrape blocks softly, starting at a height above your head, bringing them down slowly like rain falling)

> *In the middle of the night,*
> *I hear thunder,…*   (clap blocks)

> *In the middle of the night*
> *I hear a plane,…*   (scrape high and "fly" blocks like an airplane)

Ask the children what other sounds they hear at night that they would like to imitate with the sand blocks.

This activity makes a good tie-in to a unit on nighttime, or after reading a story about nighttime.

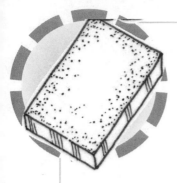

Go 'Round and 'Round the Village

This is a sand blocks version of the dancing game "Go In and Out the Window." Children enjoy singing along as they perform different actions with the sand blocks.

Sing the following song to the tune of "Go In and Out the Window":

> *Go 'round and 'round the village,* (scrape sand blocks while moving hands
> around in a circle)
> *Go 'round and 'round the village,*
> *Go 'round and 'round the village,*
> *As we have done before.*

Additional verses:
> *Go walk around the village…* ("walk" sand blocks vertically on the floor)
>
> *Go jump around the village…* (tap blocks on the floor in a jumping motion)
>
> *Go twirl around the village…* (hold sand blocks by the handles and twirl them)
>
> *Go clap around the village…*(clap sand blocks softly)

Encourage the children to think of other things for the sand blocks to do "around the village."

Sand Blocks Like to Clap

What's more fun—jumping or making a lot of noise? Most preschoolers would have a hard time choosing! With this activity, they don't have to choose—there's plenty of jumping *and* noise!

Sing the following song to the tune of "Skip to My Lou":

> *Sand blocks like to jump up and down,*
> *Sand blocks like to jump up and down,*
> *Sand blocks like to jump up and down,*
> *And then they like to CLAP!*

For the first three lines, hold sand blocks in a "standing" position and make them jump to the beat. On the word "CLAP," clap sand blocks together loudly!

Additional verses:

Sand blocks like to twirl all around,   (hold sand blocks by the handles
                                            and twirl them in the air)

Sand blocks like to twirl all around,
Sand blocks like to twirl all around,
And then they like to CLAP!   (clap blocks together loudly)

Sand blocks like to crawl on the floor,   (rub sand blocks on the floor
                                            as if they're crawling)

Sand blocks like to crawl on the floor,
Sand blocks like to crawl on the floor,
And then they like to CLAP!   (clap blocks together loudly)

Sand blocks like to scrape very softly,   (scrape sand blocks together softly
                                            while singing softly)

Sand blocks like to scrape very softly,
Sand blocks like to scrape very softly,
And then they like to CLAP!   (clap blocks together loudly)

Sand blocks like to tap tap tap,   (hold sand blocks "backward" and
                                            tap the red handles together)

Sand blocks like to tap tap tap,
Sand blocks like to tap tap tap,
And then they like to CLAP!   (clap blocks together loudly)

Activities Using Other Instruments

I've found that many rhythm instruments, while fun to play, are impractical for use by a whole class at one time, either because of noise, difficulty in playing, or expense. That is why I've developed some activities in which just one child or a few children can play at one time.

This section includes activities using cymbals, triangles, drums, and tambourines:

Cymbals combine the clapping together movement, sometimes used with sand blocks, with the brightness and resonance of metal.

Triangles make sound when a metal striker hits one of the sides of the metal triangle. Its unique sound is sweet, yet loud and resonant.

Drums come in many varieties. The activities here can be done with any drum that you hit with your hand or a mallet, or with a coffee–can drum hit with your hand.

Tambourines are lovely instruments for children. They combine the satisfying boom-boom of the drum with the delicate, tinkling sound of small cymbals.

Cymbals Introduction

Cymbals are so much fun to play! However, it would be too noisy to have an entire roomful of cymbal-banging preschoolers! One pair of cymbals can provide plenty of enjoyment.

First, show the children a pair of cymbals and demonstrate how to play them. Hold only the handles and let the cymbals wobble freely. Then quickly crash the cymbals together. Show what happens if you crash the cymbals while holding the handles too tightly, keeping the cymbals stiff. "Do they make the same sound?" Ask the children, "What would happen if you clapped the cymbals and kept them together, without bringing them apart again? Would they be louder or softer?" Try it and see.

Then pass the cymbals around the circle, allowing each child a turn to try them out.

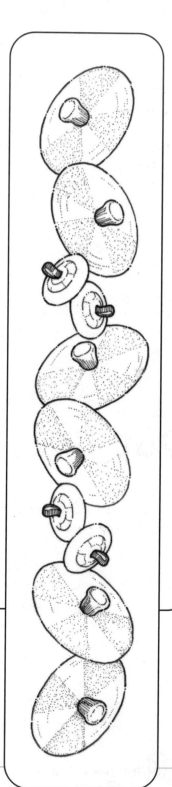

New Year's Eve Countdown (Cymbals)

This is a great activity for December 31st, of course, but it's too much fun to do only once a year. Celebrate New Year's whenever you want!

Ask the children to pretend it's New Year's Eve and they are waiting for midnight—when the New Year will begin. One child holds the cymbals. With the children, count down slowly from ten to one. Then everyone shouts, "Happy New Year!" and the child crashes the cymbals.

Play this game a few times to give several children a turn to crash the cymbals.

As a variation, the other children can hold bells or shakers and everyone can make some noise when the countdown is done!

Pop Goes the Weasel

Children should be in a circle, each in a squatting position. (It may be easier to squat starting from a standing position, rather than sitting.) One child sits in the middle of the circle, holding a pair of cymbals. Sing the following song softly:

All around the mulberry bush,
The monkey chased the weasel.
The monkey thought 'twas all in fun,
Pop! goes the weasel!

On "Pop!" the child in the middle crashes the cymbals and the other children "pop" up with a jump.

Play this game a few times to give several children a turn to crash the cymbals.

Introduction to the Drum

Drums—all kinds—are great. A nice one to use is a shallow drum with a handle that you beat with a mallet (but the kind you beat with your hands is fun, too). Good old-fashioned coffee-can drums can be a great class project. Just cover the sides of the cans with construction paper and let the children decorate them. Leave the plastic lids on the cans to be the drum heads.

Show the children a drum and all the different ways one can create sounds with it—from big booms to light taps, slow beats and fast beats. Use your hand, your thumb, your fingers, and your fist.

Pass the drum around the circle and let each child have a turn to try it out. Encourage the children to try new ways of playing the drum and be sure to admire their great ideas!

The Drum Game

The children should be standing in a circle. Explain that they will be taking slow steps when you bang on the drum slowly, "walking" steps when you play a moderate beat, and "running" steps when you play fast. Whenever you stop playing, they have to freeze like statues until you play again.

If you have a lot of space, the children can move around the room during the game. Otherwise, they can step in place while remaining in the circle.

When the children are familiar with this game, they can take turns playing the drum and leading the activity.

Animal Footsteps

This activity explores the variety of sounds you can get from a drum when you vary the rhythm, the speed, and the force with which you play it.

The children should be sitting in a circle. Pass the drum around so that each child has a turn to make "animal footsteps" on the drum. Each child can choose a different animal. Here are some ideas:

- elephant—pound drum with fist
- mouse—"scurry" fingertips on the drum
- rabbit—make fingers "hop" on the drum
- horse—pat a galloping rhythm on the drum
- snake—glide one finger around on the drum
- cat—use soft, slow taps

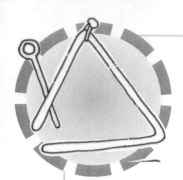

All About the Triangle

Ask the children to sit in a circle. Bring out a triangle and show the children how to play it. Hold the wooden or plastic handle that is attached to the loop that holds the triangle. Allow the triangle to wobble a bit so that the children can see how loosely it is being held by the loop. Ask the children what they think it will sound like when you strike the side of the triangle with the striker. Do they think it will be loud? Soft? Jingly?

Listen to a few responses before you strike the triangle. Did it sound the way the children thought it would?

Then ask the children what they think it would sound like if you hold the triangle in your hand when you strike it, instead of letting it wobble from the loop. "Will it sound the same or different?" Then try it. "How was the sound different from before?" Ask the children what they think it would it sound like if you put the triangle on the floor and then struck it. Try it and see.

Go around the circle and give each child a turn to play the triangle. Many will need your help holding the loop handle correctly.

All About the Tambourine

The children should be sitting in a circle. Bring out a tambourine (one with a closed, or drum-like head). Show the children some of the different ways it can be played, such as hitting it, tapping it lightly with your fingers, and shaking it. Another fun thing to do is to put it on your head like it's a hat and tap it up there!

Explain that the tambourine is like two instruments put together. Can the children guess which ones? You can hit it like a drum, but it also makes a sound when shaken, like a shaker or bells. Show how the metal disks click together when you shake the tambourine.

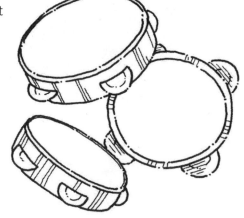

Pass the tambourine around the circle and give each child a turn to play it.

Tambourine Walk

This activity uses the two sounds of the tambourine as sound signals for different kinds of movement.

Everyone should be standing. The leader (teacher or child) plays the tambourine. The leader taps the tambourine with a regular beat. The group walks to the beat, whether slow or fast. If the leader stops, the walkers must stop and "freeze."

When the leader shakes the tambourine, this is the signal to wiggle something that the leader chooses. The leader calls out, "Wiggle your fingers!," "Wiggle one leg," or whatever he or she wishes.

Rhythm Band Activities

It requires a certain amount of maturity and discipline for young children to play as a band, with several different kinds of instruments. The children need to be able to listen carefully to know when to play their instruments, and when to stop playing. It's easy for them to get confused or distracted by the other instruments they see and hear. For this reason, rhythm band activities are generally most enjoyable and meaningful for children age four and older.

The activities in this section are designed for rhythm bands, or groups of children playing a variety of instruments. Instruments can include rhythm sticks, shakers, bells, sand blocks, cymbals, drums, triangles, tambourines, and any other instruments you have.

It's also fun to use homemade instruments such as coffee-can drums, paper plate shakers, or even pot lids banged with spoons. Enjoy a variety of sounds!

Old MacDonald's Instruments

Pass out several different rhythm instruments. It's easiest for the children if you distribute the instruments so that all the children playing rhythm sticks are sitting together, the children playing shakers are together, and so on.

Tell the children that today Old MacDonald is going to have instruments on his farm instead of animals! Remind the children that they should play only when the song tells about their instrument, so they will need to listen carefully for the name of their instrument.

Sing the following song:

Old MacDonald had a farm, e-i-e-i-o,
And on this farm he had some sticks, e-i-e-i-o,
With a tap-tap here, and a tap-tap there,
Here a tap, there a tap, everywhere a tap-tap,
Old MacDonald had a farm, e-i-e-i-o!

Additional verses:

…and on this farm he had some shakers…
With a shake-shake here, and a shake-shake there…

…and on this farm he had some bells…
With a jingle-jingle here…

…and on this farm he had some sand blocks…
With a scrape-scrape here…

…and on this farm he had a triangle…
With a ting-ting here…

…and on this farm he had a drum…
With a boom-boom here…

…and on this farm he had a tambourine…
With a shake-shake here…

…and on this farm he had some cymbals…
With a crash-crash here…

The Instruments on the Bus

Pass out a variety of rhythm instruments, keeping the children playing rhythm sticks together, the shaker players together, and so on. Remind the children that they should play only when the song names their instrument.

Sing the following song to the tune of "The Wheels on the Bus":

> *The sticks on the bus go tap-tap-tap,*
> *Tap-tap-tap, tap-tap-tap.*
> *The sticks on the bus go tap-tap-tap,*
> *All through the town.*

Additional verses:

> *The shakers on the bus go shake-shake-shake…*
>
> *The bells on the bus go jingle-jingle-jingle…*
>
> *The sand blocks on the bus go scrape-scrape-scrape…*
>
> *The triangle on the bus goes ting-ting-ting…*
>
> *The drum on the bus goes boom-boom-boom…*
>
> *The tambourine on the bus goes shake-shake-shake…*
>
> *The cymbals on the bus go crash-crash-crash…*

Rig-a-Jig-Jig

Children should be sitting in a circle. Place one pair of rhythm sticks, one shaker, one bell bracelet, one pair of sand blocks, one pair of cymbals, one triangle, one drum, and one tambourine in the middle of the circle.

Choose one child to walk around the instruments while the group claps and sings the following song:

> *As I was walking down the street,*
> *Down the street, down the street,*
> *A nice musician I chanced to meet,*
> *Hi-ho, hi-ho, hi-ho.*

At this point the child in the middle chooses one of the instruments and plays it while continuing to walk.

> *Rig-a-jig-jig and away we go,*
> *Away we go, away we go,*
> *Rig-a-jig-jig and away we go,*
> *Hi-ho, hi-ho, hi-ho.*

Repeat the game a few times to give several children a turn to walk in the middle and choose an instrument.

Sing to the traditional tune or to the tune of "London Bridge Is Falling Down."

Freeze Parade

Children should be standing in a line, parade-style. Give each child a rhythm instrument to play. (Make sure there's enough space between each child to play and march without bumping into each other.)

Put on some lively march music. Children can march to the beat around the room while playing their instruments. When you stop the music, they must "freeze" like statues. When you start the music again, the parade starts again.

As a variation, when the music stops, each child can trade instruments with another child.

Rock-a-Bye Baby

Children should sit in a circle. Pass out various rhythm instruments, one for each child.

Choose one child to curl up in the middle of the circle and pretend to sleep. (You might want to use a small blanket as a prop.)

Without playing instruments, the children sing the following song quietly:

> *Rock-a-bye baby, on the treetop,*
> *When the wind blows, the cradle will rock,*
> *When the bough breaks, the cradle will fall,*
> *And down will come baby, cradle and all.*

Wait a moment when the song ends, and then on your signal, the children pick up their instruments and play them very loudly to "wake up" the child in the middle, who can pop up as if surprised. (This should only take two or three seconds.) Then immediately give the "down" signal for the children to put their instruments down—or they'll never stop!

For extra fun, replace the word "baby" in the song with the child's name.

Play a few times to give several children a turn to be in the middle.

The Instruments in the Dell

Children should be sitting in a circle. Pass out rhythm instruments, keeping the children playing rhythm sticks together, the shaker-players together, and so on.

Ask all the children playing rhythm sticks to pick up their sticks and stand in the middle of the circle. They can tap their sticks and walk around inside the circle as the group claps and sings the following song:

> *The sticks in the dell, the sticks in the dell,*
> *Hi-ho, the derry-o, the sticks in the dell.*

Ask the rhythm sticks players to return to the circle and put their sticks down before you announce the next group.

Additional verses:

The shakers in the dell, the shakers in the dell…

The bells in the dell, the bells in the dell…

The sand blocks in the dell, the sand blocks in the dell…

The tambourines in the dell, the tambourines in the dell…

The drums in the dell, the drums in the dell…

The cymbals in the dell, the cymbals in the dell…

The triangles in the dell, the triangles in the dell…

She'll Be Tapping 'Round the Mountain

Children should be sitting in a circle. Pass out rhythm instruments, keeping the children playing rhythm sticks together, the children playing shakers together, and so on.

Before each verse, announce which instruments will be playing. For example, before the first verse, say, "Let's start with the rhythm sticks—they will be **tapping** around the mountain."

Sing the following song to the tune of "She'll Be Coming 'Round the Mountain." The rhythm sticks players should tap their sticks while the group claps and sings.

> *She'll be tapping 'round the mountain when she comes, (tap tap tap)*
> *She'll be tapping 'round the mountain when she comes, (tap tap tap)*
> *She'll be tapping 'round the mountain,*
> *She'll be tapping 'round the mountain,*
> *She'll be tapping 'round the mountain when she comes. (tap tap tap)*

Emphasize the extra "tap tap tap" beats at the end of the first, second, and fifth lines.

Additional verses:

She'll be shaking… (shakers)

She'll be jingling… (bells)

She'll be scraping… (sand blocks)

She'll be booming… (drums)

She'll be shaking… (tambourines)

She'll be tingling… (triangle)

She'll be crashing… (cymbals)

Do You Know the Jingle Bells?

Ask the children to sit in a circle. Pass out rhythm instruments in no particular order.

Without playing instruments, the children clap and sing the following song to the tune of "Do You Know the Muffin Man?":

> *Do you know the jingle bells,*
> *The jingle bells, the jingle bells?*
> *Do you know the jingle bells,*
> *Who live on Drury Lane?*

At this point, all the children with jingle bells pick up their bells, stand up where they are, and play through the end of the verse.

> *Yes, we know the jingle bells,*
> *The jingle bells, the jingle bells.*
> *Yes, we know the jingle bells,*
> *Who live on Drury Lane.*

Additional verses (repeat the two verses as above, substituting the following instruments):

> *Do you know the rhythm sticks?…*

> *Do you know the shaker kids?…*

> *Do you know the sand blocks?…*

> *Do you know the booming drums?…*

> *Do you know the triangles?…*

> *Do you know the instruments?…* (everyone plays)

Conducting the Rhythm Band

Ask the children to sit in a circle. Pass out the rhythm instruments, keeping the children playing rhythm sticks together, shaker-players together, and so on.

Put on some moderately lively music with a steady beat.

You will conduct the rhythm band, pointing and using a one-word signal (such as "sticks") to the group that you want to play. Then bring your hands up, with palms up, to indicate that they should play louder, and bring your hands down, palms facing down, to indicate that they should play more softly. Use the "And down" signal for them to stop playing and put their instruments down.

This game involves concentration on everyone's part. It's a good activity for groups who have played other rhythm band games and are ready for something a bit more difficult.

When the group is familiar with this activity, you can let the children take turns being the conductor and leading the rhythm band.

Where Are the Sand Blocks?

Children should be sitting in a circle. Pass out the rhythm instruments, keeping the children playing rhythm sticks together, shaker-players together, and so on.

Without playing instruments, the children clap and sing the following song to the tune of "Where Is Thumbkin?":

> *Where are the sand blocks? Where are the sand blocks?*

(At this point, the children with sand blocks pick them up and begin to scrape them.)

> *Here we are, here we are,*
> *We can play the sand blocks, we can play the sand blocks,*
> *Yes we can, yes we can!*

Additional verses:

> *Where are the rhythm sticks?…*
>
> *Where are the shakers?…*
>
> *Where are the jingle bells?…*
>
> *Where are the drums?…*
>
> *Where are the cymbals?…*
>
> *Where are the tambourines?…*
>
> *Where are the triangles?…*

Simon Says

Ask the children to sit in a circle. Pass out the rhythm instruments in no particular order.

Call out instructions such as "Simon says rhythm sticks play!" "Simon says rhythm sticks stop!" "Simon says bells and drums play!" and so on. Of course, if you don't say, "Simon says," the children shouldn't follow the instruction.

This game is just for fun, and no one should have to sit down or be "out" if they mess up. The confusion and silliness is part of the fun of the game.

When children are familiar with this game, you can give children turns to be "Simon" and lead the activity.

Good Activities for Toddlers

Toddlers are instinctively drawn to music—and they're always ready for fun! They are excited by the look, the feel, and the sound of rhythm instruments. With some planning and care, children in this age group can have some wonderful musical experiences playing rhythm instruments.

There are two major considerations for this age group. First, toddlers generally have not yet developed the eye-hand coordination needed to play two-handed instruments. For this reason, rhythm sticks and sand blocks are **not** recommended for toddlers.

Secondly, toddlers usually have a limited ability to play (and listen) as a group. So it is best to keep activities short, and provide simple, clear directions. Their ability to play as a group will increase with their natural development, which you can help along by offering them a regular "music time" (perhaps two or three times a week).

Shakers and bells are great instruments for toddlers. Before you start musical activities, give the children some time to become familiar with the instruments. Let them hold the instruments, turn them over, shake them, and listen to them. They will want to explore the object, the sound it makes, and how they can control that sound. Some toddlers may be hesitant to pick up an instrument and make noise. That's okay. Just leave the instrument near them—they may decide to play after a minute of watching the other children.

Safety Note: Closely supervise toddlers to make sure they do not put anything into their mouths. Also, check instruments frequently to make sure they are in good shape (e.g., no cracks, bells firmly attached, and so on).

Following are some activities that toddlers really enjoy.

Different Ways to Play. Put on some lively music with a steady, regular beat. Shake a shaker or bells to the beat and ask the children to see if they can copy you as you play in different ways, such as:

- high above your head
- tapping your shoes
- gently tapping your knees
- behind your back
- rubbing your tummy
- gently tapping your shoulders
- tapping palm of opposite hand
- rolling gently on the floor

Discuss the motions as you do them, repeating them a few times. "Can you tap on your knee?… Now we're tapping on our knee… I see Jason tapping on his knee," and so on.

Some toddlers will explore the instruments in their own ways while you do the activity. Others will enjoy trying all the different ways you show them to play.

If You're Happy and You Know It. This can be played with either bells or shakers. Most toddlers know this song and have fun adding the rattling or jingling sounds. Here are some you can try:

If you're happy and you know it, shake your bells (shaker)…
…play up high…
…rub your tummy…
…play them softly…
…play them loudly…
…tap your shoes…

Other activities elsewhere in the book that toddlers enjoy include:

Going to Kentucky (page 37)
This Is the Way We Clean the House (page 40)
Jingle Bells (page 53)
Twinkle, Twinkle, Little Star (page 55)
Bells on Ankles (page 56)
The Drum Game (page 77)
All About the Triangle (page 78)
All About the Tambourine (page 78)

Subject Index

Animals
Animal Footsteps
The Animals in the Jungle
The Cat and the Mouse
Little Jingle Mouse
Trot, Gallop, Freeze!
Wake Up, Groundhog!

Babies
Little Baby
Rock-a-Bye Baby

Celebrations
Happy Birthday Cha-Cha-Cha
New Year's Eve Countdown
The Sand Blocks Went to a Party

Circus
Circus Tricks With Bells

Colors
All About Colors

Food
Stir Up My Soup
Who Will Help Me? (The Little Red Hen)

Gardening
Digging Up a Hole

Groundhog Day
Wake Up, Groundhog!

Halloween
Walk in the Woods

Insects
The Spider Went Over the Spider Web

Night
In the Middle of the Night
Twinkle, Twinkle, Little Star

New Years
New Year's Eve Countdown

Ocean
Ocean Waves

Opposites
Shake It High and Shake It Low

Parades
Freeze Parade
Shaker Parade

Rain
I'm a Little Raindrop
Rainstorm

Seasons
Nice and Warm
Ocean Waves
Waltz of the Flowers
Wind Song

Transportation

Engine, Engine, Number Nine

The Sticks on the Bus

Tap, Tap, Tap Your Boat

The Train Is Coming

The Train Is Going Up the Hill

Windshield Wipers

Weather

I'm a Little Raindrop

Rainstorm

Wind Song

Rhythm Instrument Activities for All the Seasons of the Year

Fall

All About the Tambourine

All About the Triangle

Bells or Shaker?

Conducting the Rhythm Band

Cymbals Introduction

Different Ways to Play Bells

Different Ways to Play Sand Blocks

Different Ways to Play Shakers

Different Ways to Play Sticks

The Drum Game

Engine, Engine, Number Nine

Experiments With Shakers

If You're Happy and You Know It Tap
    Your Sticks

The Instruments on the Bus

Introduction to the Drum

Jingle Bells Introduction

"Painting" on the Floor

Rhythm Sticks Introduction

Sand Blocks Introduction

Sand Blocks Like to Clap

Shaker Square Dance

Shakers Introduction

She'll Be Tapping 'Round the Mountain
    (Rhythm Band)

The Sticks on the Bus

Sticks Up and Down

This Is the Way We Tap Our Sticks

The Train Is Coming

The Train Is Going Up the Hill

Walk in the Woods

Who Will Help Me? (The Little Red Hen)

Winter

Beethoven's 5th Symphony

Bells in Socks

Bells on Ankles

Conducting Sticks

Do You Know the Jingle Bells?

Freeze Dance With Bells

Frère Jacques

Happy Birthday Cha-Cha-Cha

Hickory Dickory Dock

In the Middle of the Night

Jingle at the Window

Jingle Bells

Little Jingle Mouse

London Bridge Letters

New Year's Eve Countdown

Nice and Warm

Old King Cole's Sticks

Rig-a-Jig-Jig

Shapes With Sticks

Stir Up My Soup

Tambourine Walk

Tapping or Scraping?

Teddy Bear Shakers

Twinkle, Twinkle, Little Star

Wake Up, Groundhog!

We're Passing Around the Bells

Spring

All About Colors

Animal Footsteps

BINGO Sticks

The Cat and the Mouse

Circus Tricks With Bells

Don't Say Ain't

Freeze Parade

Guess Who Tapped?

Hot Cross Buns

I'm a Little Raindrop

The Instruments in the Dell

Jack and Jill

Old MacDonald's Instruments

Pop Goes the Weasel

Rainstorm

Rock-a-Bye Baby

The Sand Blocks Went to a Party

Standing With Sticks

The Sticks Are Going for a Walk

Tap, Tap, Tap Your Boat

The Tapper in the Dell

This Is the Way We Clean the House

Waltz of the Flowers

Where Are the Sand Blocks?

Wind Song

Windshield Wipers

Summer

The Animals in the Jungle

Copy My Rhythm

Digging Up a Hole

Everybody Count to Six

Experiments With Sticks

Go 'Round and 'Round the Village

Going to Kentucky

I Am a Fine Musician

Jingle Around the Rosy

Little Baby

Ocean Waves

Shake It High and Shake It Low

Shaker Parade

Shakers Count to Ten

Simon Says

The Spider Went Over the Spider Web

Trot, Gallop, Freeze!

We Are Tapping

Where Is Shaker?

September

Theme _____

Activities _____ **Page Number** _____
_____ _____
_____ _____
_____ _____

Theme _____

Activities _____ **Page Number** _____
_____ _____
_____ _____
_____ _____

Theme _____

Activities _____ **Page Number** _____
_____ _____
_____ _____
_____ _____

Theme _____

Activities _____ **Page Number** _____
_____ _____
_____ _____
_____ _____

Theme _____

Activities _____ **Page Number** _____
_____ _____
_____ _____
_____ _____

October

Theme _____

Activities _____ **Page Number** ____

_____ ____

_____ ____

_____ ____

Theme _____

Activities _____ **Page Number** ____

_____ ____

_____ ____

_____ ____

Theme _____

Activities _____ **Page Number** ____

_____ ____

_____ ____

_____ ____

Theme _____

Activities _____ **Page Number** ____

_____ ____

_____ ____

_____ ____

Theme _____

Activities _____ **Page Number** ____

_____ ____

_____ ____

_____ ____

November

Theme _____

Activities

Page Number

_____ _____
_____ _____
_____ _____
_____ _____

Theme _____

Activities

Page Number

_____ _____
_____ _____
_____ _____
_____ _____

Theme _____

Activities

Page Number

_____ _____
_____ _____
_____ _____
_____ _____

Theme _____

Activities

Page Number

_____ _____
_____ _____
_____ _____
_____ _____

Theme _____

Activities

Page Number

_____ _____
_____ _____
_____ _____
_____ _____

December

Theme _____

Activities _____ **Page Number** _____

_____ _____

_____ _____

_____ _____

Theme _____

Activities _____ **Page Number** _____

_____ _____

_____ _____

_____ _____

Theme _____

Activities _____ **Page Number** _____

_____ _____

_____ _____

_____ _____

Theme _____

Activities _____ **Page Number** _____

_____ _____

_____ _____

_____ _____

Theme _____

Activities _____ **Page Number** _____

_____ _____

_____ _____

_____ _____

January

Theme _____

Activities _____ **Page Number**
_____
_____
_____

Theme _____

Activities _____ **Page Number**
_____
_____
_____

Theme _____

Activities _____ **Page Number**
_____
_____
_____

Theme _____

Activities _____ **Page Number**
_____
_____
_____

Theme _____

Activities _____ **Page Number**
_____
_____
_____

February

Theme _____

Activities
_____ **Page Number** _____
_____ _____
_____ _____
_____ _____

Theme _____

Activities
_____ **Page Number** _____
_____ _____
_____ _____
_____ _____

Theme _____

Activities
_____ **Page Number** _____
_____ _____
_____ _____
_____ _____

Theme _____

Activities
_____ **Page Number** _____
_____ _____
_____ _____
_____ _____

Theme _____

Activities
_____ **Page Number** _____
_____ _____
_____ _____
_____ _____

March

Theme _____

Activities _____ **Page Number** _____
_____ _____
_____ _____
_____ _____

Theme _____

Activities _____ **Page Number** _____
_____ _____
_____ _____
_____ _____

Theme _____

Activities _____ **Page Number** _____
_____ _____
_____ _____
_____ _____

Theme _____

Activities _____ **Page Number** _____
_____ _____
_____ _____
_____ _____

Theme _____

Activities _____ **Page Number** _____
_____ _____
_____ _____
_____ _____

Monthly Planning Pages for Rhythm Instrument Activities

April

Theme _____

Activities _____ **Page Number**

_____

_____

_____

Theme _____

Activities _____ **Page Number**

_____

_____

_____

Theme _____

Activities _____ **Page Number**

_____

_____

_____

Theme _____

Activities _____ **Page Number**

_____

_____

_____

Theme _____

Activities _____ **Page Number**

_____

_____

_____

May

Theme _____

Activities _____ **Page Number** _____

_____ _____

_____ _____

_____ _____

Theme _____

Activities _____ **Page Number** _____

_____ _____

_____ _____

_____ _____

Theme _____

Activities _____ **Page Number** _____

_____ _____

_____ _____

_____ _____

Theme _____

Activities _____ **Page Number** _____

_____ _____

_____ _____

_____ _____

Theme _____

Activities _____ **Page Number** _____

_____ _____

_____ _____

_____ _____

Monthly Planning Pages for Rhythm Instrument Activities

June

Theme

Activities

Page Number

Theme

Activities

Page Number

Theme

Activities

Page Number

Theme

Activities

Page Number

Theme

Activities

Page Number

July

Theme _____

Activities _____ **Page Number** _____
_____
_____
_____

Theme _____

Activities _____ **Page Number** _____
_____
_____
_____

Theme _____

Activities _____ **Page Number** _____
_____
_____
_____

Theme _____

Activities _____ **Page Number** _____
_____
_____
_____

Theme _____

Activities _____ **Page Number** _____
_____
_____
_____

August

Theme _____

Activities _____ **Page Number**
_____
_____
_____

Theme _____

Activities _____ **Page Number**
_____
_____
_____

Theme _____

Activities _____ **Page Number**
_____
_____
_____

Theme _____

Activities _____ **Page Number**
_____
_____
_____

Theme _____

Activities _____ **Page Number**
_____
_____
_____

Index

A

Aluminum foil, 28

B

Balance games, 59

Beans, 39

Beethoven, Ludwig von, 32

Bells, 11, 15

    for toddlers, 92

    jingle, 9, 51–62, 81–92

Birthdays, 68

Blankets, 28, 39

Blocks, 63

    Legos, 39

    sand, 9, 63–71

Body awareness, 8, 47–48, 56, 60, 62

    toddlers, 92

Boxes, 28

Bracelets, 51, 56, 59–60

C

Cardboard, 28

Cereal, 39

Circus theme, 59

Classroom tips, 10–11

Coffee cans, 56, 73, 76, 81

Coins, 39

Colors, 61–62

Construction paper, 76

Cookie sheets, 28

Cooperating, 81–90

Cotton balls, 39

Counting skills

    using cymbals, 75

    using jingle bells, 58

    using rhythm sticks, 24

    using shakers, 49

Cymbals, 73

    activities using, 75–76

    in a band, 81–90

    introduction, 74

D

Dancing

    using jingle bells, 57

    using sand blocks, 70–71

    using shakers, 37–38, 41, 43–44

Descartes, René, 7

Dramatic play

    using jingle bells, 60

    using rhythm band instruments, 85

    using shakers, 35, 37, 42, 44–49

Drums, 73

    activities using, 77

    homemade, 76

    in a band, 81–90

    introduction, 76

    toddlers, 92

F

Fine motor skills

    using jingle bells, 58

    using rhythm sticks, 14–17, 21, 26–27, 31–32

    using shakers, 36–37, 42, 45

Fucik, Julius, 59

G

Games

    Animal Footsteps, 77

    balance, 59

    Bells Tightrope Challenge, 59

    Copy My Rhythm, 23

    Copy the Child, 15

    Drum Game, 77, 92

    Freeze Dance, 57

    Freeze Parade, 84

    Guess Who Tapped? 25

    Juggling, 59

    New Year's Countdown, 75

    Peek-a-Boo, 45

    The Sand Blocks Went to a Party, 67–68

    Shapes With Sticks, 27

    Simon Says, 10, 90

    Spinning Plates, 59

    Tambourine Walk, 79

    Wake Up, Groundhog! 39

    We're Passing Around the Bells, 54–55

    Where Are the Sand Blocks? 89

    Where Is Shaker? 47

    Windshield Wipers, 31

Gardening activities, 44–45

Gross motor skills, 8

    for toddlers, 92

    using a rhythm band, 83–84

    using cymbals, 75–76

    using drums, 77

    using jingle bells, 56–57, 59, 65–68, 70–71

    using rhythm sticks, 28

    using shakers, 37–39, 41–45, 48–50

    using tambourines, 79

Groundhog Day, 39

H

Holidays. See Special days

I

Independence Day, 48

J

Jingle bells, 9, 39

    activities using, 51–62

    cautions, 91

    different ways to play, 53

    in a band, 81–90

    in socks, 56

    introduction to, 52

    on ankles, 56

    toddlers and, 91–92

    vs. shakers, 55

July 4th. See Independence Day

K

Kazoos, 11

L

Language development, 8

Legos, 39

Letter recognition, 21

Lids

    coffee can, 73, 76

    pot, 28, 181

Listening skills

    using drums, 77

    using jingle bells, 55–56

    using rhythm sticks, 22–23, 25, 29

    using shakers, 39–40

    using tambourines, 79

Literacy skills

    using rhythm sticks, 21

    using sand blocks, 61–62

M

Maracas. See Shakers

Masking tape, 59

Math skills

    using cymbals, 75

    using jingle bells, 58

    using rhythm sticks, 24, 27

    using shakers, 49

Memorial Day, 48

Music. See Musical recordings; Singing; Songs

    develops intelligence, 7

Musical recordings, 9

    25 Thunderous Classics, 59

    Beethoven's Fifth Symphony, 32

    dance, 57

    "The Entry of the Gladiators"
      by Julius Fucik, 59

    instrumental, 15, 37, 53

    John Phillip Sousa's, 48

    lively, 28–29, 56, 59, 65, 88, 92

    marches, 15, 28, 33, 48, 84

    "McNamara's Band," 48

    Preschool Playtime Band, 59

    soft, 33

    square dance, 43

    "Waltz of the Flowers" from the Nutcracker
      Suite by Piotr Tchaikovsky," 38

    "William Tell Overture" by Gioacchino
      Rossini, 29

N

Nature awareness, 44–47, 50, 62

New Year's Eve, 75

Newspaper, 28

O

Oat ring cereal, 39

Opposites

    forward and backward, 57

    loud and soft, 77

    slow and fast, 42–43, 49–50, 77

    up and down, 58, 66

P

Paper plates, 81

Peanut butter jars, 39

Pennies, 39

Pipe cleaners, 51

President's Day, 68

R

Rhymes

    "Don't Say Ain't," 27

    "Eeny Meeny Miny Moe," 23

    "Hickory Dickory Dock," 23, 58

    "Jack and Jill," 23, 33

    "Shakers Count to Ten," 49

Rhythm band instruments

    activities, 81–90

    conducting, 88–89

    tips for using, 10–11

Rhythm sticks, 9

    activities using, 13–34

    cautions, 14

    different ways to play, 15

    fluted, 13

    in a band, 81–90

    introduction to, 14

    toddlers and, 91

Rice, 39

Rossini, Gioacchino, 29

*Rubber-Band Banjos and a Java Jive Bass: Projects
    and Activities on the Science of Music and
    Sound* by Alex Sabbeth, 9

S

Safety notes
  rhythm sticks, 14
  sand blocks, 64
  shakers, 35, 40
Sand blocks, 9, 73
  activities using, 63–71
  cautions, 64
  different ways to play, 65–66
  introduction, 64
  toddlers and, 91
Sandpaper, 63
Science skills
  using jingle bells, 56
  using rhythm sticks, 28
  using shakers, 39–40, 46–47
Shakers 9, 15
  activities using, 35–50
  cautions, 35
  different ways to play, 37
  in a band, 81–90
  introduction, 36
  paper plate, 81
  toddlers and, 91–92
  vs. bells, 55
Shapes, 27
Singing. See Recordings; Songs
  children who don't, 7–8
Socks, 56
Songs
  "All About Colors," 61–62
  "The Animals in the Jungle," 46–47
  "BINGO," 20–21
  "Can You Jingle?" 60
  "The Cat and the Mouse," 29–30
  "Digging Up a Hole," 44–45
  "Do You Know the Jingle Bells?" 87–88

"Engine, Engine, Number Nine," 67
"Everybody Count to Six," 24
"Frère Jacques," 60
"Go 'Round and 'Round the Village," 70
"Going to Kentucky," 37–38, 92
"Happy Birthday Cha-Cha-Cha," 68
"Happy Birthday to You," 23
"Hot Cross Buns," 31
"I Am a Fine Musician," 24
"I'm a Little Raindrop," 50
"If You're Happy and You Know It," 18, 92
"In the Middle of the Night," 69
"The Instruments in the Dell," 85–86
"The Instruments on the Bus," 83
"Itsy-Bitsy Spider," 23
"Jingle at the Window," 57
"Jingle Bells," 23, 53, 92
"Little Baby Go to Sleep," 45
"Little Jingle Mouse," 54
"London Bridge Letters," 21
"London Bridge," 23
"Nice and Warm," 62
"Old King Cole," 25
"Old MacDonald," 82
"Pop Goes the Weasel," 75–76
"Rig-a-Jig-Jig," 83–84
"Rock-a-Bye Baby," 85
"Row, Row, Row Your Boat," 23
"Sand Blocks Like to Clap," 70–71
"The Sand Blocks Went to a Party," 67–68
"Shake It High and Shake It Low," 42–43
"She'll Be Tapping 'Round the Mountain," 86–87
"The Spider Went Over the Spider Web," 32
"Star-Spangled Banner," 23
"The Sticks Are Going for a Walk," 26
"The Sticks on the Bus," 17

"Stir Up My Soup," 42

"Tap, Tap, Tap Your Boat," 34

"The Tapper in the Dell," 26

"Teddy Bears," 49–50

"This Is the Way We Clean the House," 40

"This Is the Way We Tap Our Sticks," 15–16

"The Train Is Going Up the Hill," 66

"Twinkle, Twinkle, Little Star," 55, 92

"Wake Up, Groundhog," 39

"We Are Tapping," 22

"We're Passing Around the Bells," 54

"Where Are the Sand Blocks?" 89

"Where Is Shaker?" 47

"Who Will Help Me?" 48–49

"Wind Song" by Abigail Flesch Connors, 41

Sousa, John Phillip, 48

Spatial concepts, 8

    forward and backward, 57

    high and low, 42–43

    up and down, 16–17, 58, 66

Special days

    birthdays, 68

    Groundhog Day, 39

    Independence Day, 48

    Memorial Day, 48

    New Year's Eve, 75

    President's Day, 68

    St. Patrick's Day, 48

    Teddy Bear Day, 49–50

Spoons, 81

St. Patrick's Day, 48

Stories

    "The Little Red Hen," 48–49

    "Rainstorm," 20

    "Walk in the Woods," 18–19

    "Windshield Wipers," 31

T

Tambourines, 73

    in a band, 81–90

    introduction, 78

    toddlers and, 92

Tchaikovsky, Piotr, 48

Teddy Bear Day, 49–50

Time, 58

Toddlers

    activities for, 91–92

    safety notes, 91

Towels, 28

Trains, 65–67

Triangles, 73

    activities using, 79

    in a band, 81–90

    introduction, 78

    toddlers and, 92

V

Velcro, 51

W

Weather, 50

"What if?" questions, 10

Whistles, 11

Winter, 62

Wiggle Giggle & Shake

200 Ways to Move and Learn
Rae Pica

Enhance your classroom with 200 movement-inspiring activities for children ages four to eight. Explore 38 popular classroom themes such as holidays, nature, animals, nutrition, and more. This book offers simple, practical, and fun movement activities and ideas grouped according to these popular themes. 192 pages. 2001.

ISBN 978-0-87659-244-1
Gryphon House | 19284

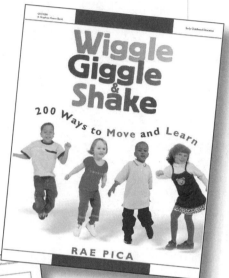

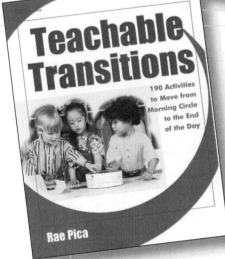

Teachable Transitions

190 Activities to Move from Morning Circle to the End of the Day
Rae Pica

Filled with movement activities, games, fingerplays, chants, and songs, *Teachable Transitions* transforms the transitions between planned activities into pleasurable moments children look forward to! The activities, organized by arrival, departure, snack, outside time, naptime, and cleanup, help children move through their day. Theme connections link to the curriculum, adding continuity and more opportunities for learning. With its "Ready, Set, Go" format, transitions become fun, stress-free learning moments. 144 pages. 2003.

ISBN 978-0-87659-281-6 / Gryphon House
14658

Also
Available

Do You Know the Muffin Man?

Literacy Activities Using Favorite Rhymes and Songs
Pam Schiller and Thomas Moore

Teach literacy with over 250 familiar songs, rhymes, and activities!

Rhyme, rhythm, and music are an essential part of a quality early childhood program. The authors of the perennial favorite, *Where is Thumbkin?* have created activities children will love to accompany the 250 rhymes and songs in this invaluable new literacy book. Children learn letter recognition, vocabulary, phonemic awareness while they are singing and rhyming. Each rhyme or song includes theme connections so teachers can easily add literacy and music into their daily plans. 256 pages. 2004.

ISBN 978-0-87659-288-5 / Gryphon House 19624

The I Can't Sing Book

For Grownups Who Can't Carry a Tune in a Paper Bag But Want to Do Music with Young Children
Jackie Silberg

Who says you need an opera singer's voice to teach music to young children? Fascinating, easy activities help even the most tone-deaf adult show children the wonder and magic of making and hearing music. All you need are rubber bands, paper clips, jingle bells, paper plates and other everyday items to bring the joy of music to children. 174 pages. 1998.

ISBN 978-0-87659-191-8 / Gryphon House / 15921

Also Available

Literacy Play

Dramatic Play Activities That Teach Pre-Reading Skills
Sherrie West and Amy Cox

Children love to pretend, and dramatic play is the perfect environment for practicing and applying literacy concepts. Whether they decide to be firefighters, to open a pet store, or to have a tea party, children will increase their vocabulary, communicate with their friends, and learn to recognize environmental print—all important skills for pre-readers. *Literacy Play* is chock-full of creative dramatic play activities that teach important pre-reading skills while bringing children's imaginations to life! 256 pages. 2004.

ISBN 978-0-87659-292-2 / Gryphon House 17548

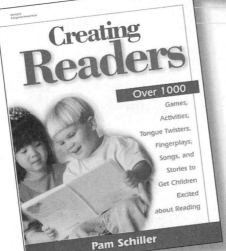

Also Available

Creating Readers

Over 1000 Games, Activities, Tongue Twisters, Fingerplays, Songs, and Stories to Get Children Excited About Reading
Pam Schiller

Learn the basic building blocks of reading with *Creating Readers,* the comprehensive resource that develops a strong foundation for pre-readers. *Creating Readers* gives teachers and parents tools to teach pre-reading skills with over 1000 activities, games, fingerplays, songs, tongue twisters, poems, and stories for the letters of the alphabet. These simple games and activities help children learn the sound of every letter of the alphabet. This invaluable resource develops a child's desire to read as well as the skills needed to begin reading. *Creating Readers* starts children ages 3 to 8 towards a future rich with books and reading. 448 pages. 2001.

ISBN 978-0-87659-258-8 / Gryphon House / 16375

The Complete Book of Rhymes, Songs, Poems, Fingerplays, and Chants

Over 700 Selections
Jackie Silberg and Pam Schiller

Build a strong foundation in skills such as listening, imagination, coordination, and spatial and body awareness with over 700 favorite rhymes, songs, poems, fingerplays, and chants. 500 pages. 2002.

ISBN 978-0-87659-267-0
Gryphon House | 18264

The Complete Book of Activities, Games, Stories, Props, Recipes, and Dances

For Young Children
Pam Schiller and Jackie Silberg

Award-winning authors Pam Schiller and Jackie Silberg team up to bring you the ultimate resource! Bursting with new selections and old favorites, each of the 600 activities, stories, games, recipes, props, and dances will enhance any preschool curriculum. Companion to *The Complete Book of Rhymes, Songs, Poems, Fingerplays, and Chants*, it is an essential addition to every classroom! Includes a materials index, theme connection index, and a thematic chart that explains how to use the book to round out any curriculum. 512 pages. 2003.

ISBN 978-0-87659-280-9 / Gryphon House / 16284

Also Available

The GIANT Encyclopedia of Theme Activities for Children 2 to 5

Over 600 Favorite Activities
Created by Teachers for Teachers
Edited by Kathy Charner

This popular potpourri of over 600 classroom-tested activities actively engages children's imaginations and provides many months of learning fun. Organized into 48 popular themes, from dinosaurs to the circus to outer space, these favorites are the result of a nationwide competition. 511 pages. 1993.

ISBN 978-0-87659-166-6
Gryphon House / 19216

The GIANT Encyclopedia of Art & Craft Activities for Children 3 to 6

More Than 500 Art & Craft Activities
Written by Teachers for Teachers
Edited by Kathy Charner

A comprehensive collection of the best art and craft activities for young children. Teacher-created, classroom-tested art activities to actively engage children's imaginations! The result of a nationwide competition, these art and craft activities are the best of the best. Just the thing to add pizzazz to your day! 568 pages. 2000.

ISBN 978-0-87659-209-0
Gryphon House / 16854

The GIANT Encyclopedia of Circle Time and Group Activities for Children 3 to 6

Over 600 Favorite Circle Time Activities
Created by Teachers for Teachers
Edited by Kathy Charner

Open to any page in this book and you will find an activity written by an experienced teacher for circle or group time. Filled with over 600 activities covering 48 themes, this book is jam-packed with ideas that were tested by teachers in the classroom. 510 pages. 1996.

ISBN 978-0-87659-181-9
Gryphon House / 16413

The GIANT Encyclopedia of Science Activities for Children 3 to 6

More Than 600 Science Activities
Written by Teachers for Teachers
Edited by Kathy Charner

Leave your fears of science behind as our *GIANT Encyclopedia* authors have done. Respond to children's natural curiosity with over 600 teacher-created, classroom-tested activities guaranteed to teach your children about science while they are having fun. 575 pages. 1998.

ISBN 978-0-87659-193-2
Gryphon House / 18325